Foreword

One of the great pleasures of being involved in education is the satisfaction derived from contributing to the intellectual growth of students. Further gratification occurs by witnessing students' contributions beyond the educational experience. The Marine Corps War College's faculty and staff are more than blessed by interacting with students who have already proven themselves as tremendous leaders. Each year, our seminars are filled with top performers from all the services, government agencies, and international partners. Those students are prepared to cross a threshold into the strategic realm and move into senior leadership positions or senior advisory roles. It is the mission of the War College to better prepare them to serve the country in those positions by stimulating critical thought and by challenging their previously held beliefs.

Our relatively small size compared to our fellow War Colleges allows unparalleled access, agility, and personal educational opportunities. We have exceptional access to senior leaders and leverage this access by fitting the entire student body into the senior leader's conference room where they engage in a free dialog with that leader. Our students have recently met with the Secretary of Defense, the Chairman of the Joint Chiefs of Staff, the Secretary of Homeland Defense, members of Congress, the Director of the FBI, and the National Security Advisor, among others. They also engage with non-governmental notables such as the Council on Foreign Relations, JP Morgan, advertising giant J Walter Thompson, traders on the New York Stock Exchange, and a wide variety of media outlets, to name just a few.

The students benefit from a first-rate faculty with whom they interact on a daily basis on a close, professional level, creating unique learning opportunities. The War College is proud to host guest professors, speakers, conferences, and exercises that increase that diversity of thought. Many lessons are put into the curricula specifically to challenge what would be considered mainstream thought.

The Marine Corps War College promotes bold, innovative thought and academic freedom. That philosophy is encouraged and enabled by the leadership at Marine Corps University, which provides an environment in which scholarly discourse—even regarding topics that might be unpopular or controversial—can flourish in accordance with the precepts of academic freedom. In fact, the War College welcomes controversy, for controversy sows the seeds of creativity and exposes students to divergent opinions. The Marine Corps War College does everything in its power to not only present differing points of view but cultivate innovative ideas.

Our faculty is also constantly evolving the curriculum to ensure relevance while maintaining the use of enduring educational principles. The college strives to strike a balance between current debates and timeless ideas. The study of war and its causes is at its essence the study of human nature and human interaction. Our curriculum and interactive teaching philosophies are specifically designed around metacognition, thinking about how you think, and the impact thinking processes have on decision-making. Rather than teaching what to think, we stress how to think. When that evolution occurs, the faculty and staff of the Marine Corps War College have fulfilled their mission. The essays that are included in this anthology are evidence of just that—bold ideas that should spark debate as the United States enters this new era of persistent conflict.

Michael F. Belcher, Col USMC
Director, Marine Corps War College

Robert J. Mahoney, Ph.D.
Dean, Marine Corps War College

Preface

U.S. Army Chief of Staff George Casey coined the phrase "era of persistent conflict" to describe the world we face in the 21st century. Adjectives abound for the future environment in which U.S forces, civilian and military, will operate in years to come: complex, uncertain, dynamic, and decentralized, to name a few. The types of operations that the men and women of the U.S. government must be prepared to conduct run the gamut from major combat operations (MCO) to counterinsurgency (COIN) to humanitarian operations. Although to some these debates and operations seem as if they have sprung from the cauldrons of Afghanistan (Operation Enduring Freedom [OEF]) and Iraq (Operation Iraqi Freedom [OIF]), they are anything but new.

From the 1980s through today, the names for these operations have changed: low intensity conflict (LIC); small-scale contingencies (SSC); military operations other than war (MOOTW), operations other than war (OOTW); stability operations and support operations (SOSO, which an Army officer I interviewed several years ago claimed "perfectly captured how the Army felt about the mission"); stability and support operations (SASO); stability and reconstruction operations (S&RO); and stability, security, transition, and reconstruction operations (SSTRO), the latest incarnation thanks to Department of Defense Directive 3000.05, which mandates that stability operations become a core U.S. military mission.

Many of these terms prove dangerous for several reasons. First, in the case of MOOTW and OOTW specifically, defining an operation by what it is *not* provides little intellectual, let alone operational, clarity. Second, since these operations were not identified as war (i.e., the military's core competency) they were undervalued across the DOTMLPF (doctrine, organization, training, material, leadership, personnel, and facilities) spectrum. Third, as soldiers, sailors, airmen, and Marines soon discovered in OEF and OIF, definitional differences between war and "other operations" become blurred on the ground. Fourth, one does not always get to pick the operation type that will serve a particular national end. The enemy, or host population, gets a vote.

More U.S. service personnel have lost their lives in SSTROs than in strictly defined MCOs since the Korean War. To the soldier on the ground, being in a MOOTW looked little different at times from being in an MCO, and certainly was as deadly. And as every National Security Strategy since 9/11 correctly identified, existential threats could stem from mission failures beyond MCOs—the inability to conduct successful SSTROs could result in failed states, ungoverned territories, and terrorist havens. Planes crashing into the Twin Towers, Pentagon, and a field in Pennsylvania demonstrated what may initiate from failed or failing states. In other words, it is no longer a given that the U.S. military can afford to screw up SSTROs so long as it gets the "big one" right.

The students who come to the Marine Corps War College (MCWAR) have gracefully endured an operational tempo unprecedented in world history by an all volunteer force. A nation in two hot wars and a global campaign against violent extremism should be commended for providing its officers time for professional military education, and the country will reap huge dividends from its investment. As many have said, this conflict will not be won with bullets or the numbers killed in action. New solutions and ideas warrant careful consideration.

This edited volume contains the type of ingenuity that the United States needs at this critical juncture in its history. If we are at the threshold of an era of persistent conflict, U.S. leaders must consider unique capabilities, organizations, and missions to be successful. Even U.S. culture may need to adapt—if conflict is truly persistent, we may need to foster more resiliency than currently may exist in our culture. This volume takes a new look at capabilities, organizations, and missions in this era of persistent conflict, and closes with an analysis of how ultimately the country's fate rests with its people, and the implications for that analysis.

This volume of papers begins with one of the central strategic issues facing the country—the lack of operational, deployable civilians. Many studies on ideal solutions to grow civilian capacity gather dust on credenzas. Until this utopian ideal is realized, however, the United States desperately needs to fill this gap with civilians trained, organized, and equipped to operate in these environments alongside their military counterparts, as Christie LaPlume writes in chapter one, "Plugging the Gap: A Comparative Review of Variables that Affect Civilian Deployment Capacity." LaPlume's innovative research took her to seven civilian agencies that currently deploy to war zones in an attempt to identify best practices that can be immediately implemented. For her outstanding efforts, LaPlume received MCWAR's 2010 best paper award.

Chapter two by John C. Vara continues the exploration

of civilian capacity, specifically by assessing and proposing alternatives to the State Department's Office of the Coordinator for Reconstruction and Stabilization (S/CRS). The organizational analysis continues with Doug M. Hammer's call to establish a U.S. Stability Operations Command in chapter three. Harvey R. Robinson and Matthew G. St. Clair then examine missions that have new import yet historical roots in chapters four and five, on security force assistance and anti-piracy operations, respectively. Fritz W. Pfeiffer's chapter six uses Carl von Clausewitz's trinity (emotion, chance, reason) to look at strategic decision-making in this era of persistent conflict, using the decision to go to war in Iraq in 2003 as a case study. The book concludes with Roger R. Laferriere's call for a National Risk Communications Strategy that would ultimately make the U.S. population more resilient to future attack in this era of persistent conflict. Laferriere's groundbreaking analysis earned him MCWAR's 2009 best paper award.

No silver bullet will end the wars in which the United States is engaged, and none of these papers contain one. This book is intended to initiate, rather than end, discussion. If any of the ideas in these papers contribute to making the country better able to navigate the next era, the U.S. government's men and women whose thoughts are contained herein will be, in part, the beneficiaries, as will a grateful nation.

Spanning two academic years, the works in this anthology would not be possible without the unfailing support of the Marine Corps University. Three successive University Presidents supervised and supported the production of this anthology: Major General (Retired) Donald R. Gardner, Lieutenant General Robert B. Neller, and Major General Thomas M. Murray. Each, in turn, championed critical and creative thought throughout the University, thus perpetuating an educational environment which demanded academic rigor while promoting academic freedom. Thanks also to the librarians and staff of the University's General Alfred M. Gray Marine Corps Research Center, who so superbly and selflessly assisted our students in their research. We are likewise eternally grateful to the U.S. Marine Corps History Division and Marine Corps University Press, whose expertise and experience were essential in guiding this project from concept to completion.

Special thanks also goes to MCWAR's faculty who so conscientiously mentored the design, development, research, and writing of these research projects. Recognizing that scholarly knowledge only flourishes under the light of public scrutiny, the faculty championed for the creation of a new venue to showcase these works and expose them to a wider audience. They were the intellectual midwives for the first edition of the MCWAR Papers and the works contained herein. Behind the scenes, the Director, Colonel Michael F. Belcher, and Dean of Academics, Dr. Robert J. Mahoney, provided the vision, guidance, and encouragement required for this project to reach a successful conclusion.

Lastly, our heartfelt gratitude is extended to The Basic School, which provided junior officers to augment the College staff and aid this project. Working with minimal guidance or supervision, Second Lieutenant Adam P. Backsmeier, with assistance from Warrant Officer One Aaron T. Hladik, edited this volume. Displaying the utmost talent and tact, these officers worked tireless with the authors and editor to bring organizational clarity and grammatical correctness to this work.

***

The views expressed in this book are those of the authors and do not reflect the official policy or position of the U.S. Government, Department of Defense, United States Marine Corps, Marine Corps University, or the Marine Corps War College.

Dr. Tammy S. Schultz
Professor, Marine Corps War College

Contents

Plugging in the Gap:
A Comparative Review of Variables that Affect Civilian Deployment Capacity

by Christie E. LaPlume

ABSTRACT

Focus beyond federal agencies that are normally thought of as those involved in reconstruction and stability operations is needed when it comes to legislation improving civilian deployment capacity. The variables that affect civilian deployment capacity to a war zone are shared by all federal agencies no matter what mission is pursued. Seven federal agencies pursuing various U.S. national security objectives in Afghanistan were chosen for a comparative review.

This comparative review was conducted to illustrate two points. One, that good practices exist and if shared, are potentially applicable to all agencies for fixing short-term gaps in civilian deployment capacity and two, that discrepancies that erode civilian deployment capacity exist beyond the scope officially explored to date. Civilian deployment protocols are compared and contrasted, "best" practices are proposed, and suggestions for new incentives are introduced.

Emphasis is placed on the fact that discrepancies in benefits can erode civilian volunteerism to serve in war-zones. If legislation is to be considered and passed to benefit civilians and civilian deployment capacity, more comprehensive studies on the existing differences need to be conducted, to include studies on the short- and long-term effects of war-zone deployment on civilians, their families, their mental health, and effects on retention rates in federal government service.

A Personal Note

The subject of this article was, in part, inspired by personal experience. As a civilian federal employee, I volunteered for two tours to Afghanistan—one for a 12-month commitment in Bagram in 2007-08, and another for a three-month commitment at a remote base in the northern Konar/southern Nuristan areas of operation in 2008-09. In both locations, I was exposed to various other U.S. Government agency employees who had also volunteered to work in Afghanistan to fulfill their respective agency missions.

During brief periods of interaction—either when our missions had cross-purpose or when we attended U.S. military meetings upon request as interagency representatives – it was evident that there were varying degrees of exposure to and experience working with the U.S. military; varying degrees of continuity in representation; varying degrees of Afghan-specific expertise; and often times competing agency mission priorities. Most apparent was that we were all deployed for different lengths of time, with different benefits and career goals, with a wide-variety of professional experiences and backgrounds. It made me curious about how each agency attracted its volunteers, how the preparation and processing were similar or different, and whether or not the ground experience gained during deployment was used to further each respective agency's mission.

With this context I decided to compare and contrast the civilian deployment protocols of various agencies active in Afghanistan. In order to sustain civilian deployment capacity for the foreseeable future in Afghanistan, as well as to other venues as required, it seemed prudent to look for variables that affect capacity for deployment as well as to identify and share between the agencies any good practices that emerge. Good or best practices, once identified, can be used as models for all agencies faced with a long-term civilian deployment requirement, ongoing or in the future.

Finding very little in terms of available printed material on this subject, the research for this article required personal interviews with various points of contact within each agency compared. I soon learned that there was no single "expert" on war-zone deployments within each department/agency; the variables that I chose to compare required talking to both administrative and operational components in each department/agency. Unfortunately, I was unable to talk to all the contacts that I could have or should have for the optimal comparative study. The term "review" was substituted for "study" to convey that this article just scratches the surface of the issues, and perhaps does not cover the expanse of variables that affect civilian deployment capacity. As I quickly realized, there were a lot of nuances to be further explored that I was unable to pursue. As was concluded in a Government Accounting Office study that was published in September 2009 (GAO-09-1019T), the variations in incentives, medical benefits, and tracking of civilian employees can affect morale and long-term viability for deploying civilians to war zones. This review tries to show that differences and discrepancies in benefits exist over and beyond those studied by the GAO to date and any legislation or permanent changes to civilian deployment incentives or benefits should be considered after comparing all federal agencies, not just those involved in reconstruction and stabilization operations.

The time given and hospitality shown to me by each and every agency representative kind enough to give me insight into their respective agency practices was much appreciated. These individuals should be applauded for their tireless efforts behind the scenes to meet the challenge of deploying civilians to conflict areas for without them, our civilian deployment capacity and our ability to pursue our national security interests abroad would be significantly limited.

THE CIVILIAN GAP

The U.S. military experience in the two contemporary war-zones of Iraq and Afghanistan highlighted the need for quick growth in civilian deployment capacity, specifically for conducting reconstruction and stability operations. In 2005, the U.S. State Department was designated to coordinate this effort, but after five years the task remains daunting. In this context, numerous government studies reviewed civilian pay incentives and medical-related benefits looking for ways to create and promote civilian deployment capacity.[1]

The latest study, conducted by the Government Accounting Office in 2009, compared six federal agencies involved in reconstruction and stability operations and concluded that inequities in benefits would undermine civilians' willingness to volunteer for war-zone duty.[2] Based on this conclusion, the Office of Personnel Management was tasked to propose legislation standardizing some aspects of civilian compensation.[3]

Focus beyond federal agencies involved in reconstruction and stability operations is needed when considering legislation to improve civilian deployment capacity. The variables that affect deployment capacity to a war-zone are shared by all federal agencies no matter what mission is pursued. Indeed, in complex operations, many missions are likely to be pursued simultaneously. Seven federal agencies pursuing various U.S. national security objectives in Afghanistan were chosen for a comparative review. The review was conducted to illustrate two points. One, that good practices exist and, if shared, are potentially applicable to all agencies for enhancing civilian deployment capacity. Two, benefit discrepancies erode civilian will to volunteer for deployment continue to exist beyond the scope officially studied to date.

The seven agencies are introduced with a brief overview of war-zone missions and general deployment protocols for baseline knowledge. Specific protocols for a set of variables associated with civilian deployment are then compared and contrasted. Protocols of the most experienced of the seven agencies vary and are relatively robust; they evolved over time based on respective agency-specific experience and lessons learned. Protocols of relatively new federal agencies deploying civilians to war-zones are still being tested. Practical solutions for managing civilian deployment are identified as potential "best practices" applicable to all agencies. These "best practices" may help fill in short-term gaps in civilian deployment capacity if and when they occur, now or in the near future, until more permanent solutions are found.

This comparative review highlights the need for a more formal study of civilian-based deployment variables in order to ensure long-term viability for civilian deployment. It also suggests the need to search for new and innovative incentives, proposing a few ideas in an attempt to create interest and momentum on this critical subject. Finding solutions to filling in civilian deployment gaps, whether short or long term, is vital to ensuring a robust and whole-of-government ability to pursue U.S. national security interests overseas.

WAR ZONE MISSIONS AND GENERAL PROTOCOLS FOR CIVILIAN DEPLOYMENT

Seven agencies with substantial experience in deploying civilians overseas have both similarities and significant differences in how civilian employees are deployed to Afghanistan. References to a tour in Afghanistan vary from "war-zone" to "unaccompanied tour" to "hardship post." No matter the label, each agency has successfully met and maintained their respective civilian deployment requirements collectively for over nine years, suggesting they have adopted successful deployment protocols and policies within their own organizations.

The Department of State (DOS) is the forerunner to all agencies conducting overseas missions and hosts all U.S. Government (USG) agencies that operate overseas. Foreign Service Officers (FSOs) promote U.S. foreign policy and play a key role in seeking conflict resolution through non-kinetic solutions to best serve U.S. interests.[4] FSOs serve at American Embassies abroad for a standard tour of two years with accompanying family. These tours are considered a permanent change-of-station (PCS). Where living conditions and safety are compromised, PCS tours are unaccompanied and shortened to one year.[5] Unaccompanied tour vacancies are managed by respective regional components that sponsor these types of tours and the "bidding process"[6] for these tours is held separately and prior to bidding for standard tours in the attempt to fill them first. The Family Liaison Office (FLO) has advocacy and support oversight for officers designated for all unaccompanied tours, war-zone or not.

The Department of Defense (DOD) has deployed civilians alongside U.S. Military (USMIL) personnel in combat throughout its history.[7] Today, despite functional differences in their mission sets, DOD civilians, no matter for which agency they work, are regulated under the same Departmental policies.[8] Despite a universal approach, slight differences in personnel-related protocols occur between DOD agencies pending mission and agency-specific requirements. Included in this review are three DOD agencies with relatively large numbers of deployed civilians to Afghanistan.

The National Security Agency "provide[s] direct support to combat elements, [specifically] cryptological collection and analysis for U.S. national defense and homeland security."[9] Deployed personnel include not only technical operators but also administrators, support, and logistics officers. Although war-zone vacancies are sponsored by a variety of operational and administrative offices, oversight for selection and processing of deployment candidates is centralized under two entities: the Mission Operations Center (MOC) and the Global Deployment Center (GDC),[10] both established in 2006. Most war-zone positions are temporary duty (TDY), although PCS tours are growing.[11]

The National Geo-Spatial Intelligence Agency (NGA) provides "direct combat support by developing imagery and map-based intelligence solutions for U.S. national defense, homeland security, and safety of navigation as well as...global support to Intelligence Community mission partners through NGA representatives stationed around the world."[12] War-zone vacancies are integrated into an internal, general vacancy database but a centralized Deployment Review Board selects from applicants for deployment. Civilian deployment is limited to TDY tours only. Since 2006, advocacy and support oversight is consolidated under the Expeditionary Operations Directorate.

Defense Intelligence Agency (DIA) officers are "major producers and managers of foreign military intelligence that is provided to war fighters, defense policymakers and force planners in the Department of Defense and the Intelligence Community, in support of U.S. military planning and operations and weapons systems acquisition."[13] Deployment vacancies are advertised and filled by each component that sponsors war-zone positions. Civilian deployments are limited to 179-day TDY tours. War-zone deployment efforts were standardized with the 2004 establishment of the DIA/Readiness Center.

Department of Justice law-enforcement representation abroad spans a history of over six decades.[14] The rise of global terrorism and crime in the 1990s[15] increased the overseas presence exponentially as liaison with foreign counterparts was established to coordinate international leads and to exchange information.[16] With its poppy production and history of harboring Al-Qai'da key leaders, Afghanistan gives the Federal Bureau of Investigation (FBI) and the Drug Enforcement Administration (DEA) ample reason and purpose for extensive representation.

The FBI mission,[17] war-zone or not, is "to protect and defend the United States against terrorist and foreign intelligence threats, uphold and enforce the criminal laws of the United States and provide leadership and criminal justice service to federal, state, municipal, and international agencies and partners."[18] The Office of International Operations, International Fusion Cell (IFC), established in 2004, manages personnel deploying to any war-zone.[19] Prior to 2004, various tactics to maintain deployment capacity were used and found inadequate.[20] Deployment candidate selection was an informal, very selective process based on profiling agents with U.S. military experience. Today, war-zone candidates compete as candidates for all field positions, in a transparent, rigorous, and competitive application process.[21] Conversion of TDY positions in Afghanistan to one-year PCS assignments is in process.

The DEA steady state mission is "to enforce the controlled-substances laws and regulations of the United States and to bring to justice organizations involved in the growing, manufacture or distribution of such substances,"[22] amongst additional related goals. War-zone deployments are managed by regional components.[23] War-zone vacancies are integrated into a general vacancy database and candidates are chosen based on qualifications and experience. Typical PCS tours are three years; for Afghanistan, tour length is two years with the option to extend for a third year. The DEA was mandated to significantly increase its presence in Afghanistan by late 2009 and had little difficulty doing so.[24] Additional personnel include permanent year-round TDY billets for Foreign-deployed Advisory and Support Teams (FASTs).[25]

The Central Intelligence Agency (CIA) mission, war-zone or not, is to "provide national security intelligence to senior US policymakers"[26] by collecting and reporting human-derived intelligence (HUMINT), providing and disseminating all-source reporting and analysis, and providing overall intelligence support to Ambassadors, U.S. military commanders, and other relevant USG entities.[27] War-zone vacancies are integrated with general vacancies in an in-house vacancy database. Selection and administrative processing of deployment candidates is conducted by the area or functional component that sponsors the position.

SPECIFIC DEPLOYMENT VARIABLES COMPARED AND CONTRASTED

Due to sensitivities of some agencies to disclose human resourcing specifics, the below comparisons minimize agency identifiers where possible, introducing some specific deployment protocols in each of the categories below, with the ultimate goal of identifying trends that affect civilian deployment capacity over time without compromising USG agencies or departments.

Candidate Selection

Most agencies integrate war-zone vacancies into general vacancy databases. Volunteer opportunities thus require a comprehensive search, combing through vacancies for all regional and functional components. A few agencies list war-zone vacancies separately, making it relatively easier to find, and even compare, war-zone volunteer opportunities. Most agencies advertise war-zone vacancies year-round as positions come vacant, and selection of candidates is made by the various regional and functional components that sponsor the war-zone positions. One agency, although selection is ultimately made by regional and functional components, advertises war-zone vacancies ahead of standard vacancies in an effort to fill the war-zone vacancies first. This allows the agency to prioritize and identify critical gaps and work to fill them prior to filling more traditional vacancies.[28] Differences in how positions are advertised do not appear to impact the ability of an agency to fill war-zone vacancies; no agency is experiencing significant gaps in volunteer candidates.

With regard to strategies that have been used to temporarily fill gaps in volunteers, one agency announces internal "surges" when needed, requiring offices who are least affected by the requirement for volunteers to provide officers for lateral duty to the offices and locations where volunteers are needed.[29] In-house surges and influx of personnel allows those with appropriate expertise to deploy while "surged" personnel on a temporary basis cover headquarters-centric duties. The surges create situations for identifying new, potentially willing, deployable officers.

Meanwhile, one agency maintains a "retired cadre"[30] hired as independent contractors when needed to temporarily fill some war-zone positions. These officers have a lifetime of agency-specific experience and are an organic reserve capability if, or when, needed.

No candidate selection process in this limited review definitively ensures that the right volunteers apply or get deployed. All but one agency has a policy requiring minimum on-the-job experience as criteria for deployment. In general, intelligence agencies have shorter experience criteria than that required by law enforcement agencies—one to two years minimum experience compared to six to seven years minimum experience, respectively. Meanwhile, intelligence agencies, on average, deploy a greater number of employees to the war-zone than law enforcement agencies. A correlation seems to occur between the number of positions and number of years of experience—the more civilians needed to fulfill war-zone vacancies, the lower the general experience-level required.

None of the compared agencies requires prior military service or prior experience working with the U.S. military. Minimal practical experience, or lack of direct experience with USMIL does not appear to have any effect on success and/or early return from war-zone deployments.[31] Short-of-tour issues, on average, have been related to unanticipated domestic situations that required the presence of the employee back in the United States or egregious behavior, not necessarily related to lack of skill-based knowledge or technical experience.

Universally, younger, newer employees volunteer more readily and more often. A general lack of commitment to location, a mortgage, or family can explain this trend. One positive outcome of younger, newer employees deploying to war-zones is the relatively low ratio of subordinates to managers. A close working and living environment affords enhanced opportunities for new officers to be mentored and to develop team-building skills.

On the other hand, war-zone as a first work experience can temper expectations and condition work habits that do not correspond with respective agency cultural or professional standards after redeployment. The quick work tempo and pace of learning work-related skills in a war-zone can have several effects, including exposure to greater responsibilities more quickly than if working at a routine position at a respective Headquarters. Also, due to the need for field-expedient solutions in a war-zone, cutting corners can undermine norms that were taught during training.[32] These scenarios can have a demoralizing or ostracizing affect for the relatively new employee upon re-integration.[33] A frustrating experience can also have a negative effect when considering the characteristics of "Gen-Xers" who are apt to change careers more often than previous generations.[34] There are no studies on long-term effects on retention of employees whose first experience is in a war zone.[35]

Motivations/Incentives

The top three motivators for federal civilians to deploy to a war-zone are (in order): 1) financial entitlement; 2) a sense of patriotism; and 3) potential for career enhancement.[36] The aforementioned 2009 GAO study[37] compared pay incentives of six federal agencies involved in civilian reconstruction and stability operations and found inequities that would undermine long-term willingness to deploy based on varying pay scales.[38] Discrepancies in bonus amounts offered by agencies also exist.

Within the intelligence community (IC), deployment bonuses vary significantly.[39] One agency provides a flat rate of $5,000 for every six months served in a war-zone while another agency provides an $8,000 bonus for six months of service with graduated amounts that increase as more time is served. Whereas one agency provides $10,000 accumulatively for a one-year PCS tour, some deployed civilians are collecting up to $20,000 during a one-year period by completing multiple TDY tours. Within one intelligence agency, bonuses differ pending skill sets—volunteers with a particular skill set are less apt to volunteer and, therefore, a larger bonus is offered as enticement; meanwhile, a subset of employees with a different skill set and a larger volunteer pool receives a lower bonus.[40]

Civilian war zone veterans who responded to surveys expressed great job satisfaction and deemed personal sacrifices made to serve their agency and country were worthwhile.[41] Career enhancement was less of a guarantee. The expectation for preferential consideration for future tours and promotions was oftentimes not met, although this was usually the result of timing and not due to lack of trying by respective agencies.[42] For one particular agency, serving in a war zone was an option to "buy" additional time toward career when otherwise the officer was on the verge of forced resignation.[43]

No evidence suggested that recognition for war-zone duty is expected by personnel who deploy, but most agencies present returnees with certificates and medals in formal acknowledgement of their service and anecdotally, the recognition is appreciated.[44] Most recently, the DOS established a medal for dependent children in recognition of the sacrifice that families make during extended separations.

Although ultimately there was no evidence of agency-hopping, or severe lack of volunteers based on discrepancies between agencies in deployment incentives and practices, the potential for negative effects on morale due to lingering discrepancies is important when considering sustainment of civilian deployment capacity.

Tour Lengths

The majority of agencies offer PCS tours. Only one agency limits civilian deployments to TDY-only, although multiple TDY tours are permitted. Although TDY tours are easier to fulfill in the short-term, keeping up capacity long-term poses a challenge since TDY positions are not back-filled (i.e., no one takes over the position while the individual is deployed). This may be the reason that some agencies are aspiring to convert TDY tours to PCS positions.[45]

Several agencies, based on anecdotal information, note increased divorce rates related to prolonged deployment. It is unclear, however, as to whether or not divorce was due to the separation created by deployment or if deployment exacerbated stresses and tendency toward divorce already in play prior to deployment.[46] This trend has been examined and verified in studies on U.S. military personnel.[47] Adverse affects, however, on civilians from prolonged deployments have not been studied.

Depending on the agency, tour length dictates the number of rest and recreation (R&R) entitlements, if any. Policies on where R&Rs can be taken and how long they last differ amongst the seven agencies. In the end, variations in tour lengths and R&R entitlements did not appear to affect ability to fill war zone vacancies although, like financial entitlements, discrepancies could have a corrosive effect over time.

Pre-Deployment Preparation and Training

All agencies require a physical exam for war-zone candidates; only a few require a mental health interview. All agencies require area-familiarization training ranging from one to two weeks. None have mandatory language requirements; none have training related to working with translators. A few agencies rely on the DOS or DOD pre-deployment courses although the majority have independent programs, tailored to their specific mission and personnel. All agencies require varying levels of proficiency on a variety of weapons using various in-house ranges, trainers, and training schedules. One agency employs the use of a firearms simulator, onsite, in the vicinity of its deployment center. Some agencies require training in tactical driving skills as well as first aid.

Surveys noted that civilians from at least two agencies felt they were well prepared for deployment.[48] Clinical evidence suggests that the more mentally-prepared an employee is with the realities of living and working conditions in a particular situation, the more tolerable and successful that employee will be no matter how adverse the conditions.[49] If personnel are aware beforehand, for example, that they will be using communal facilities, they are able to set their expectations appropriately. Getting to their deployed location and finding out after the fact of the hardships involved can easily undermine morale and make one feel as if they were "duped" into deploying. This, in turn, will undermine deployment capacity in the long run. Most agencies have opportunities for sharing war-zone experiences peer-to-peer.[50]

Although the availability of any of the above training does not, in itself, appear to affect civilian deployment capacity, it does show that there is a large contract environment for providing war-zone affiliated tactical training for civilians. Many of these civilians will serve side-by-side in the war zone, yet they are trained by assorted instructors for varying lengths of training to different proficiency levels at various locations. The inability to keep pace of training with the number of deployment candidates for one agency, at one time, caused a back-log of personnel in need of training. This ultimately slowed down the flow of deployment, causing gaps between when personnel departed the war-zone and when their replacements arrived. In fact, no agency appears to have insurmountable difficulties in finding suitable, deployable personnel. Rather, managing the timing, availability, and completion of training of a selected candidate to match the rotation of a pending vacant position is the challenge.

Family Support

According to a report focused on the USMIL community,[51] soldiers felt better if assured a good support system was available to their families during their deployment, underscoring the importance of strong family support programs. Taking this as a cue, civilian agencies work hard to make personnel and family support robust and accessible.[52] DOD civilians often have access to programs available to USMIL personnel, although eligibility varies with different service policies.[53] Universally, all agencies assess their programs routinely to improve family out-reach and available support services. Web-sites, literature, and other resources on war-zone deployment are available for employees and their families.[54] A fact that was prominently noted by most federal agency war-zone coordinators is the paucity of studies or empirical data on the effects to civilians exposed to war-zone environments—short or long term, making identification of needs and provision of assistance problematic.

One exclusive benefit to civilians allowing them to reconnect with their families is the number of opportunities to depart the war-zone during a PCS assignment on R&R.[55] R&R opportunities are evaluated as critical[56] yet the policies related to R&R opportunities vary amongst the civilian agencies.

Post-Deployment and Re-Integration

Many agencies require post-deployment physicals and at least two agencies, a mandatory post-deployment mental health interview. Some agencies attempt to gain feedback from returning officers, although only two have conducted significant surveys on deployment experiences, and responses were voluntary. Only one agency has a clear cut way of gaining mandatory feedback. Upon return from each and every deployment, officers are required to fill in a pre-determined questionnaire with space for optional feedback. This data is captured in a unique war-zone database. All monetary benefits associated with the deployment are held until the questionnaire and critical feedback are provided.

Re-integration is relatively easy for personnel filling TDY tours; employees return to their positions which are not back-filled during their absence. Agencies that sponsor only TDY tours create a challenge for themselves, however, because it is difficult for employees to pursue multiple tours as their absence can create a negative impact on the home office ability to conduct its mission. Additionally, Afghanistan-gained experience might be lost if not applied upon re-integration. By all accounts, every agency attempts to give preferential consideration for onward assignments for those who serve PCS in war-zones. Timing of rotation, however, can affect availability and vacancy of onward "choice" assignments.

PROPOSED "BEST" PRACTICES

Candidate Selection

A centralized approach to both selection as well as processing of deployment candidates ensures consistency and synergy to the deployment experience, ultimately benefiting both the deployed and their sponsors. Recruitment and selection of best candidates is necessary for effective mission accomplishment. However, this can be especially challenging for war-zone vacancies given the financial incentive that motivates some toward volunteering. Oversight for coordinating efforts between disparate operational and functional offices that sponsor war-zone vacancies, in theory, optimizes communication and maximizes a whole-of-agency effort to finding the best candidates for deployment. Unlike agencies that deploy relatively large numbers of personnel in a decentralized selection environment, the use of a "clearing house," in effect, keeps less suitable deployment candidates from eventually finding a position for which they might get selected based solely on lack of candidates for that vacancy.

A war zone-dedicated database where all vacancies as well

as other administrative tasks are centrally accessed and managed provides an easy, one-stop-shopping experience for those who are interested in volunteering. The centralized approach to processing all candidates for the duration of their deployment—from pre-, during, and post-deployment phases—is a proven method for tracking personnel with war-zone experience and capturing important data associated with their experience. Positive experiences foster positive attitudes and willingness to continue to volunteer.[57]

Incentives

Standardizing as many variables with regard to incentives and benefits as possible decreases inequities associated with shared experiences amongst federal agency civilians who deploy and work side-by-side with USMIL, facing the same risks. Meanwhile, new and innovative incentives should be explored, such as: offering low- or no-interest loans to civilian veterans for higher educational purposes—for self or family members; allowing the designation of leave donation to a spouse, child, or parent if all are USG employees; centralizing USG medical processing or oversight for civilian veterans, perhaps taking advantage of existing DOD facilities and capabilities; extending tax benefits to civilians.[58] Making these benefits equitable is not only the right thing to do—it is the smart thing to do if this deployable capacity is to grow, and be sustainable.

Tour Lengths

No clear-cut best practice emerged related to tour length although anecdotally there is a one-year tolerance for the majority of civilians who volunteer for high-stress work environments.[59] One agency was the exception in establishing a longer PCS standard that might be reconsidered if maintenance of deployment capacity or health issues specific to Afghanistan arises.

R&R policies should be standardized in order to minimize perceived inequities. Different approaches to tour lengths should be considered. For example, a time-share approach to war-zone positions might ease the burdens of separation for some members of the general population. This concept involves two or three employees sharing a position between field and Headquarters on a rotational basis, allowing maximum flexibility on timing and du-

ration of stay in either venue with a schedule coordinated between the employees and the stakeholders of both positions. This
bifurcated approach to mission accomplishment allows for effective application of field experience and maximum pursuit of area
expertise.

Pre-Deployment Preparation and Training

Mental preparation for living and operating in a war-zone
is essential.[60] A good practice is to promote the sharing of "war
stories" and experiences between "veterans" and deployment candidates.[61] Many agencies do this through brown bag lunches and
round table seminars. Understanding the realities of living in a
war-zone sets expectations, exponentially increasing the probability of completing a successful full-term tour.[62]

Access to a firearms simulator provides opportunities to
practice and become more proficient on a skill that is required but
offered with limited exposure. Although a few agencies share
training opportunities, the majority of the firearms and tactical
training as well as area-familiarization are done in-house, by each
agency, for its respective deployment candidates. One potentially
good practice or change with regard to war-zone training would
be the consolidation of training centers and instructors. This
training could be standardized according to general mission set.
For instance, all intelligence entities could standardize area-familiarization training so that all intelligence personnel are working from the most comprehensive information available while all
law-enforcement entities could standardize and consolidate tactical and operational training. This suggestion is made due to the
number of civilian employees from different agencies who find
themselves working side-by-side, in the same locations, facing the
same risks with vastly different skill levels. Therefore, working
knowledge and training should be standardized.

There is potential to enhance and encourage inter-agency
coordination by exposing various agency officers to each other
prior to deploying, and possibly working together in the field, by
consolidating some of the training—offering weapons training
on the same weapons at the same location by the same instructors
to the same proficiency standards. Consolidating some of the
training is one way to possibly address the financial cost associ-

ated with civilian deployment and deployment capacity-building as well.

Family Support

All agencies are aware of the importance of providing support to families when civilian volunteers deploy for either TDY or PCS tours. Inclusion of family members or significant others in select pre-deployment seminars reinforce organizational commitment to families. Variations and extent of family outreach can make a difference, but one of the most important aspects of family support is ensuring communication capability is available for the deployed to communicate with family and friends. Another is related to benefits, such as R&R, and health care being on par with military counterparts. Presence of a war-zone advocate ensures agency-wide compliance and awareness of war-zone issues.

Post-Deployment and Reintegration

Several good practices are worth noting. Mandating a period of leave upon return from deployment allows for complex re-acclimation to social and work norms.[63] Inclusion of family members in select post-deployment seminars encourages recognition that separation is a two-way experience, enhancing the probability for a successful re-acclimation process. Public recognition through ceremonies and issuance of awards instill a sense of organizational appreciation, as well as contextualizing the patriotic experience. Tying benefits to completion of mandatory post-deployment protocols ensures compliance.[64] Mandatory medical and mental health interviews upon return will allow for better collection of data and tracking of civilian employees if, or when, health conditions are discovered. Lastly, offering awareness training to managers on deployment-related trends to better empathize with and mentor war-zone veterans goes a long way in integrating civilian deployment capacity as a whole-of-agency responsibility.

PLUGGING IN FUTURE GAPS

This comparative review only scratches the surface of exploring similarities and differences amongst varying protocols from a subset of federal agencies deploying civilians to war-zones.

The GAO recommendation to address inequities in civilian incentives and benefits is a start in addressing discrepancies that can undermine long-term civilian will to volunteer for war-zone duty.[65] An attempt to highlight "best practices" in order to mitigate future short-term gaps in civilian deployment capacity led to other areas worth exploration. These include looking for new and innovative incentives to broaden the pool of current civilian volunteers, considering consolidation of weapons and orientation training, as well as centralization of the monitoring and treatment of civilian physical and mental health issues.

Unlike the U.S. military,[66] there is insufficient study of the effects on the mental health of civilian employees from war-zone deployments. The U. S. military's ability to universally track soldiers and their medical data collected before and after deployments is robust. No equivalent process or effort exists for federal civilian personnel. This is significant as U. S. military personnel are conditioned for combat, yet are still experiencing high levels of post-combat stress, whereas civilians are not trained for war yet the effects on their mental health are unknown. The GAO has looked at this issue in depth,[67] but it is not clear that its recommendations are sufficient. Although "civilian combat veteran" is a copyrighted term[68] for commercial purposes, the concept is worth exploring with regard to setting parameters that define whether, and if so when, civilians are entitled to the same benefits extended to U.S. service members. More thorough studies are warranted if the United States intends to maintain, not to mention grow, civilian deployment capacity for the future.

It is incumbent upon the U.S. Government to understand all the variables that effect civilian deployment to war-zones in order to build and maintain capacity for long-term deployments in the future, potentially to multiple locations. Failing to do so can eventually limit the ability to effectively pursue national security objectives and, ultimately, to protect U.S. national security interests from abroad during times of conflict.

Notes

[1]U.S. Government Accountability Office, *Human Capital: Improved Tracking and Additional Actions Needed to Ensure the Timely and Accurate Delivery of Compensation and Medical Benefits to Deployed Civilians,* testimony, September 16, 2009, before the U.S. House, Subcommittee on the Federal Workforce, Postal Service, and the District of Columbia, Committee on Oversight and Government, (Washington DC: GAO, 2009). Also available online: http://www.gao.gov/new.items /d091019t.pdf. U.S. Government Accountability Office, *Deploying Federal Civilians to the Battlefield: Incentives, Benefits, and Medical Care,* April 2008, U.S. House, Subcommittee on Oversight and Investigations, Committee on Armed Forces (Washington DC: GAO, 2008). Also available online: http://armedservices.house.gov/pdfs/Reports/CiviliansonBattlefieldReport.pdf. U.S. Government Accountability Office, *DOD Civilian Personnel: Medical Policies for Deployed DOD Federal Civilians and Associated Compensation for Those Deployed,* testimony, September 18, 2007, before the U.S. House, Subcommittee on Oversight and Investigations, Committee on Armed Forces (Washington DC: GAO, 2007). Also available online: http://www.gao.gov/new.items/d071235t.pdf. U.S. Government Accountability Office, *DOD Civilian Personnel: Greater Oversight and Quality Assurance Needed to Ensure Force Health Protection and Surveillance for Those Deployed,* September 2006, Report to Congressional Committees (Washington DC: GAO, 2006). Also available online: http://www.gao.gov/new.items/d061085.pdf.
[2]GAO, *Human Capital,* 10.
[3]Ibid., 9. See also Allysa Rosenberg, "Agencies Seek to Standardize Pay and Benefits for Civilians Overseas," *Government Executive,* April 14, 2010, http://www.govexec.com/story_page.cfm?filepath=/dailyfed/0410/041410ar2.htm&oref=search.
[4]"Foreign Service Officer," *U.S. State Department,* http://careers.state.gov/officer/.
[5]Unaccompanied Tour Support Officer (Family Liaison Office, Department of State), interviewed by author, Washington DC, January 12, 2010. All interviews for this chapter were conducted under anonymity and the names of the interviewees are withheld by mutual agreement.
[6]State Department officers go through a bidding process for positions; when ready to rotate from one position to another, six bids for six separate positions are submitted through an HR process. The offices that sponsor the vacancies then consider and select officers for the position from the bids that are submitted.
[7]"History: Civilians Supporting Our National Defense," *U.S. Army: Civilian Personnel On-Line (CPOL),* April 1, 2009, http://acpol.army.mil/employment /about_history.htm.
[8]David S. C. Chu, "Memorandum on Building Increased Civilian Deployment Capacity," *Department of Defense Directives Program,* February 12, 2008, (Washington DC: 2008). Also available online: http://www.dtic.mil/whs/directives/ corres/pdf/pr080212capacity.pdf; GAO, *Deploying Federal Civilians,* Appendix E.

[9]"About NSA," *National Security Agency*, http://www.nsa.gov/about/index.shtml.

[10]Chief of Global Deployment Center (National Security Agency), interviewed by author, Washington DC, January 27, 2010. Whereas the Global Deployment Center facilitates administrative processing for deploying personnel the Mission Operations Center represents the operational side of deployment, managing the various operational components and their respective candidate selection processes. This "one-stop-shopping" approach to processing personnel for deployment ensures consistency in applying deployment protocols, limiting variations and possible discrepancies from potentially divergent deployment protocols of the many operational sponsors.

[11]Ibid.

[12]"About," *National Geospatial-Intelligence Agency*,https://www1.nga.mil/About/Pages/default.aspx.

[13]Chief of the Readiness Center (Defense Intelligence Agency), interviewed by author, Washington DC, January 18, 2010. Due to difficulty in finding replacements, the Director of the DIA recently mandated that all personnel deployed TDY remain in place until a designated replacement is identified and enroute; this was intended to motivate all aspects of "the system"—the deployed, the "losing office", the "gaining office" and personnel officer—to continuously and actively find TDY volunteers.

[14]"Legal Attache Offices: History," *Federal Bureau of Investigation*, http://www2.fbi.gov/contact/legat/history.htm.

[15]Ibid.

[16]Ibid.

[17]Special Agent (Federal Bureau of Investigation), interviewed by author. Per interview with senior FBI Special Agent who has served intermittently in Afghanistan since 2003, the FBI's mission in Afghanistan started out primarily focused on counter-terrorism (CT) operations, interviewing captured enemy combatants and foreign detainees, looking for evidence to bring certain terrorists to justice for their roles in past events that targeted U.S. personnel and property. Today, the FBI has a three-fold strategy in Afghanistan: the continuation of its traditional CT mission; counter-intelligence and criminal investigations within the expanded USG community; and, building indigenous capacity in domestic intelligence collection. The FBI provides mentorship in forensics and other counter-crime and corruption methods and law enforcement issues. A major focus, in this latter area, is training and mentoring of Afghan security force officers assigned to the newly created Major Crimes Task Force (MCTF).

[18]"Other Agencies on Mission's 'Country Team,'" *U.S. Diplomacy: An Online Exploration of Diplomatic History and Foreign Affairs,* U.S. Diplomacy, http://www.usdiplomacy.org/state/abroad/countryteam.php.

[19]Chief of an International Fusion Cell (Officer of International Operations, Federal Bureau of Investigation), interviewed by author, FBI Headquarters, Washington DC, March 12, 2010.

[20]Ibid. One such tactic was to assign deployment duty on a rotational basis to various FBI domestic operational components. It was thought at the time that strong teams would form from existing units, minimizing the timeframe needed

to acclimate to conditions in a hostile work environment. Although team members worked well amongst themselves their skill sets, training, and knowledge-base oftentimes did not match what was needed to fulfill FBI's tactical and strategic goals on a consistent basis in the war zone.

[21]Ibid.

[22] "Mission's 'Country Team,'" U.S. Diplomacy.

[23]Acting Section Chief (Office of Global Enforcement) and Supervisory Special Agent (Office of Global Enforcement at the Drug Enforcement Administration), interviewed by author, DEA Headquarters, Arlington, VA, March 17, 2010. Personnel deployed to Afghanistan are processed by the regional component within DEA that has Afghanistan and Pakistan in its purview while personnel deployed to other hardship posts may be processed by other regional components (i.e. Iraq is managed by the regional component that also has purview over Turkey).

[24]Ibid. Whereas the first deployment wave consisted of 13 DEA officers, the numbers of required officers recently increased to 81 including special agents, intelligence analysts, program specialists and diversion investigators. There were approximately 100 applicants for the 52 special agent vacancies.

[25]DEA also has permanent TDY billets worldwide for their Foreign-deployed Advisory and Support Teams (FASTs) which deploy, depending on ops-tempo and location, for 90-120 day durations on a constant rotational basis, to assist foreign partners in conducting counter-narcotics operations. For Afghanistan, the establishment of a FAST rotation was mandated to commence as of September 30, 2009. There, FASTs work side-by-side with USMIL as well as Afghan security forces and are deployed for 120-days.

[26]"About CIA," *Central Intelligence Agency*, https://www.cia.gov/about-cia/index.html.

[27]*Central Intelligence Agency*, U.S. Code 50 (2010), §403-4 and -4a.

[28]Department of State officers bid for positions, normally submitting six top choices in order of preference. Bids for positions take place twice a year, during normal rotation periods in the summer and in the winter. Bidding for unaccompanied tours, to include war-zones, take place prior to the two routine bidding timeframes.

[29]Information provided during multiple interviews with personnel involved with CIA deployment processing.

[30]Greg Miller, "Spy Agencies Outsourcing to Fill Key Jobs," *The Los Angeles Times*, September 17, 2006; Anthony R. Williams, "CIA Support to Enduring Freedom," *Military Intelligence Professional Bulletin*, Oct-Dec 2002. Although not confirmed, this practice is a good idea for not only filling war-zone vacancies on a temporary basis but also for filling other staff employee gaps when needed.

[31]During interviews with all agency representatives, all noted few "short-of-tour" issues.

[32]Discussed anecdotally between interviewer and several of the agency representatives interviewed.

[33]As a result of successfully handling the pace and responsibilities gained in a war-zone, the younger, less-experienced officers upon return to their headquarters tend to get promoted quicker (one form of preferential treatment); this can

be demoralizing to an older cadre of officers to work for a younger, less-experienced officer, or it can be demoralizing to the new employee as expectations might be inflated. Based on early promotion in career, expectation may be for quick promotions in future.

[34]Penelope Trunk, "What Gen Y Really Wants," *Time Magazine*, July 05, 2007, http://www.time.com/time/magazine/article/0,9171,1640395,00.html#ixzz0jc vXWnLF. Statistics on "Gen X"ers indicate the tendency to change careers, on average, more than seven times during their lifetime.

[35]Rutzick, Karen, "Taxing Duty," *Government Executive*, May 11, 2006, http://www.govexec.com/story_page.cfm?filepath=/dailyfed/0506/051106pb.h tm&oref=search.

[36]Department of State 2007 Survey; a 2009 unpublished intelligence agency survey and supporting anecdotal feedback from all seven agency representatives interviewed.

[37]GAO, *Human Capital*, 10.

[38]Ibid., 6-9; For example, some deployed civilians are paid on the Foreign Service (FS) pay scale while others are paid on the General Schedule (GS) pay scale; different pay scales have different parameters dictating overtime, danger pay, and other aspects of salary that can significantly differ.

[39]Based on interviews with representatives of four intelligence agencies—CIA, NSA, NGA, and DIA.

[40]Former PEMS officer, interviewed by author, March 9, 2010.

[41]2007 State Department survey.

[42]Ibid. and 2009 unpublished survey of an intelligence agency.

[43]Department of State has an "up or out" protocol for senior officers who do not get promoted within a five year of making senior grade; if during the five year period the officer bids for an unaccompanied, hardship tour, they are eligible to extend that review period by the amount of time spent in that tour.

[44]Discussed during some of the interviews conducted with agency representatives on the subject of formal recognition for personnel following a war-zone tour.

[45]FBI and DEA are converting many of their TDY positions in Afghanistan to PCS positions. NSA is also increasing their number of PCS tours.

[46]Clinical psychiatrist, interviewed by author, March 18, 2010. Discussed during dialogue with clinical psychiatrist involved with conducting pre- and post-deployment interviews of civilians associated with one particular agency. Also, briefly touched upon with various interviewees who are familiar, through internal anecdotes within their agencies, related to divorce and deployments.

[47]American Psychological Association Presidential Task Force on Military Deployment Services for Youth, Families, and Service Members, *The Psychological Needs of U.S. Military Service Members and Their Families: A Preliminary Report*, (February 2007), 26.

[48]2007 State Department survey; 2009 unpublished survey from an intelligence agency.

[49]Psychiatrist, interview, March 18, 2010. The clinical psychologist was employed with an agency that required pre- and post-deployment mental health

interviews and who has interviewed many war-zone returnees in the course of his responsibilities.

[50]During interviews with representatives from five of the seven agencies, several practices were shared in which those seeking to volunteer in war-zones had opportunities to meet with those who had already served; many of the agencies shared the same type of practice of conducting brown-bag lunches, open houses, seminars, etc.

[51]Senior Advisor (Expeditionary Operations Directorate, National Geospatial-Intelligence Agency), interviewed by author, NGA Headquarters, Reston, VA, January 14, 2010.

[52]Agency representatives that were interviewed provided pamphlets and resource material that is available to deployment candidates and their families; many provided many details associated with ways that their respective agencies were improving ways to support family members.

[53]Ibid. For example, the U.S. Army allows 16 hrs of free drop-in childcare per child, per family, per month at designated Family Childcare Centers during operating hours; families of civilians deployed with the U.S. Army are eligible to participate. Meanwhile, the U.S. Air Force provides two-hour childcare on a monthly basis, at a pre-determined time, date, and place for the families of deployed military personnel; civilian families are not eligible to participate.

[54]Currently, an informal attempt on a quarterly basis to share these resources amongst inter-agency HR and war-zone representatives is hosted by DOS.

[55]Information provided anecdotally from several of the interviewees; visits not only recharged their batteries but also they spent more quality time with family and friends than prior to deployment.

[56]Psychiatrist, interview, March 18, 2010. Anecdotal information suggests that many civilians deployed to war-zones found R&Rs recharged their batteries making prolonged separation from families more tolerable; many commented on more quality time with family compared to when they were at their CONUS jobs.

[57]Psychiatrist, interview, March 18, 2010. Also, conclusion of GAO, *Human Capital* supports this intuitive theory.

[58]Many senators have attempted to gain tax benefits for civilians but to no avail; the issues that keep this legislation from passing should be studied/pursued; blogs on this subject show great interest and passion with regard to this benefit.

[59]Psychiatrist, interview, March 18, 2010.

[60]Ibid.

[61]Ibid.

[62]Ibid. and results from a 2009 unpublished survey of civilians conducted by one federal agency with 50 percent respondent rate.

[63]APA, *Psychological Needs*, 30.

[64]Tying benefits to completion of protocols can also ensure tracking and accountability with regard to civilian physical and mental health issues, thorough collection of deployment statistics, and opportunity for providing invaluable feedback loop.

[65]GAO, *Human Capital*, 9-10.

[66]APA, *Psychological Needs,* 23-25.

[67]GAO, *Human Capital,* 9-10. This source noted that civilians deployed to war zones are eligible for treatment at USMIL medical facilities although this entitlement was not well communicated to all civilian agencies nor is well-understood amongst U.S. Military care givers. Recommendations included enhancing communication for better understanding of the status quo entitlement.

[68]"Trademark Electronic Search System: Civilian Combat Veteran," *United States Patent and Trademark Office,* August 14, 2007, http://tess2.uspto.gov/bin/show-field?f=doc&state=4010:1s2nbn.2.1.

National Security and the Interagency Enterprise: A Critical Analysis

by John C. Vara

ABSTRACT

This chapter argues that the U.S. interagency foreign-service apparatus is flawed. The current concept of coordinating interagency operations under the State Department's Office of the Coordinator for Reconstruction and Stabilization (S/CRS) cannot work effectively because S/CRS does not have the required authority or operating framework to meet its coordination responsibilities across the interagency community. For any U.S. government department or agency to effectively coordinate and direct interagency operations, it must have a congressional mandate, authority, and funding through legislation.

Two options are examined as possible solutions. First, the State Department's Office of the Coordinator for Reconstruction and Stabilization (S/CRS) could work effectively as the interagency coordinator if it receives congressional authority similar to what FEMA received through the Stafford Act. The United States Agency for International Development (USAID) is also examined. It too is deemed to be an effective candidate as the interagency coordination hub. Like S/CRS, it would also need congressional authorities and an operational framework derived from legislation. USAID has the advantage of a strong legacy in foreign assistance and an expeditionary culture. For these reasons and more, USAID should be the primary candidate for coordinating and directing the interagency process in the context of foreign-service, and foreign assistance and development.

INTRODUCTION

> *America's interagency toolkit is a hodgepodge of jerry-rigged arrangements constrained by a dated and complex patchwork of authorities, persistent shortfalls in resources, and unwieldy processes.*
> —Robert Gates, Secretary of Defense, Speech at Nixon Center, February 24, 2010.

Today's international security environment requires an interagency, whole-of-government approach in order to provide security both at home and abroad.[1] This whole-of-government concept is often referred to simply as "the interagency" and implies that there is a homogenous organization channeling the capabilities of various government organizations toward a single goal with unified effort. The fact is, however, there is no such organization and by its very nature, interagency activities do not harmonize.[2] Individual agencies have their own core missions with their own agendas and requirements. There is no unity of command, no clear delineation of authority or institutional incentive for effective cooperation, let alone collaboration.[3] The current interagency apparatus lacks meaningful mechanisms to unify its effort, learn lessons, build doctrine, or gain a common cultural perspective.[4] The net result is a failure to effectively "operationalize" the broad notion of the interagency at the practitioner level and to build an effective bureaucratic system that can provide responsive, dependable, and repeatable services to support national foreign policy interests and homeland security.[5]

Harnessing the whole of national power through interagency cooperation has challenged the United States for decades and is strikingly similar to the challenges faced by the U.S. military as it wrestled with unification and then joint-service cooperation over the last 70 years.[6] Despite the differences, one can make useful comparisons between today's interagency process and the challenges faced by the U.S. military over the past decades. Just like the military's struggle with joint-service cooperation, the U.S. interagency apparatus will not realize its full potential until Congress provides clear legal authority, mandates a functional and effective bureaucratic framework, and guarantees adequate funding through legislation. Only then, with an authoritative organizational framework, will the United States be able to effectively administer interagency collaboration and project the totality of its national powers.[7]

In building a case for a congressionally mandated and authoritative interagency apparatus, this chapter examines the current framework for interagency coordination and will draw conclusions and make recommendations for a better way to operate.

THE "INTERAGENCY"

The term "interagency" describes the collaborative effort of various government agencies to merge their unique capabilities and focus them toward a single goal in a unified effort. Over the years the Defense Department (DOD), State Department (DOS) and U.S. Agency for International Development (USAID) have developed a habitual relationship and are best understood as partners. In contrast, domestic agencies have not developed any habitual relationship with the defense and foreign services.[8] The term "whole-of-government" is often used to identify the collection of domestic government agencies that are called upon to assist the foreign-service and military with foreign assistance, development and/or reconstruction and stabilization. This chapter uses the terms interagency and whole-of-government interchangeably.

One could argue that a coherent interagency capability has existed in the past. The Marshall Plan after World War II (WWII), the U.S. International Cooperation Administration in the 1950s, and later USAID in the 1960s all serve as historical examples.[9] During Vietnam, the Civil Operations and Revolutionary Development Support (CORDS) Program aimed to win hearts and minds while today, Provincial Reconstruction Teams in Iraq and Afghanistan are engaged in building infrastructure, creating markets, generating commerce, and establishing governance.[10] Additionally, one can point to embassy country teams abroad or disaster relief efforts at home (Hurricane Katrina) to make the case that the interagency is alive and well—and is not a new concept.

All that said, these examples actually support the thesis that the interagency is at the very least inefficient, if not dysfunctional. While some of these programs had relative success, some were near disasters. USAID, for example, has a long history and an impressive resume of accomplishments. But today, it is simply a broker for foreign aid and currently operates with limited operating resources and manpower.[11] The interagency response for Hurricane Katrina, on the other hand, was notably bad and sparked a congressional investigation to find out what went wrong.[12] Provincial Reconstruction Teams (PRTs), civil-military teams deployed to Afghanistan and Iraq, have not fared much better, with a Congressional investigation revealing serious shortfalls.[13] Embassy country teams, collections of personnel from various U.S. government agencies, also come up short. Although these teams fall under the ambassador's (or chief of mission) supervision and bring a mix of capabilities and competencies together, country team members often pursue narrow agency agendas. The ambassador charged with oversight may, or may not, have any experience in leading such an operational team, a problem compounded by the team's wide charge that ranges from market analysis and expansion, business development, law enforcement and intelligence gathering.[14] In sum, the U.S. interagency experience is, at best, a mixed bag.

THE INTERAGENCY PROCESS

Interagency policy coordination for foreign assistance is the responsibility of the National Security Council (NSC) with the State Department acting as the lead cabinet department for coordination of action, namely through S/CRS and USAID.[15] The 1947 National Security Act gave the National Security Council the statutory responsibility to coordinate interagency policy while the State Department was designated the lead cabinet for coordinating stability operations by National Security Presidential Directive 44 (NSPD-44). Each will be briefly examined in turn.

In 1947 Congress reorganized the entire United States National Security Apparatus. During the time after World War II and on the brink of the Cold War, both the executive and legislative branches recognized that the United States needed to reform its security posture. The 1947 National Security Act realigned the military establishment, consolidated the national intelligence effort creating the Central Intelligence Agency and created the National Security Council.[16] The National Security Council is the President's principle advisory group for strategic policy and is not subject to

NATIONAL SECURITY COUNCIL ORGANIZATION

	Office of the Secretary of Defense	Joint Staff	Department of State	Other Executive Branch
National Security Council	Secretary of Defense	Chairman of the Joint Chiefs of Staff	Secretary of State	President, Vice President, Secretary of the Treasury, Assistant to the President for National Security Affairs, Director of Central Intelligence, Chief of Staff to the President, Assistant to the President for Economic Policy, Attorney General, Director OMB, Counsel to the President
Principals Committee	Secretary of Defense	Chairman of the Joint Chiefs of Staff	Secretary of State	Secretary of the Treasury, Director of Central Intelligence, Chief of Staff to the President, Attorney General, Director OMB, Counsel to the President, Chief of Staff to the Vice President, Assistant to the President and Deputy National Security Advisor, and others as required
Deputies Committee	Deputy Secretary of Defense or Undersecretary for Policy	Vice Chairman of the Joint Chiefs of Staff	Deputy Secretary of State	Assistant to the President for National Security Affairs and other deputies of Principals

POLICY COORDINATION COMMITTEES (PCCs)

PCCs–Regional	Europe and Eurasia Western Hemisphere
	East Asia South Asia
	Near East and North Africa Africa

PCCs–Functional	Democracy, Human Rights, and International Operations
	International Development and Humanitarian Assistance
	Global Environment
	International Finance
	Transnational Economic Issues
	Counterterrorism and National Preparedness
	Defense Strategy, Force Structure, and Planning
	Arms Control
	Proliferation, Counterproliferation, and Homeland Defense
	Intelligence and Counterintelligence
	Records Access and Information Security

Senate oversight. Each president issues an updated Presidential Policy Directive-1 (PPD-1) which allows every President to tailor the NSC role and responsibilities within his administration.[17]
National Security Council Organization – Joint Publication 3-08 pg II-4 [18]

In addition to its advisory role, the NSC also serves to integrate national security policy across domestic, foreign, military, and intelligence domains. Together with supporting interagency working groups, high-level steering groups, executive committees, and task forces, the NSC provides the foundation for interagency coordination.[19] Although the council initiates the development of national security policy, it does not normally implement policy. Rather, the NSC continually coordinates and monitors the interagency policy process to ensure that the President always has appropriate policy options available and monitors the execution of the President's policies. The nature and degree of NSC involvement in this policy process depends on the President's desires.[20]

The U.S. national security policy starts with the National Security Council drafting the National Security Strategy (NSS).[22] Once signed by the President, the National Security Strategy guides policy development, and integrates and coordinates all the instruments of national power in order to accomplish national objectives.[23] Within this strategic body, the Interagency Policy Committees manage the day-to-day activities of interagency coordination of national security policy.[24] Evaluating the U.S.

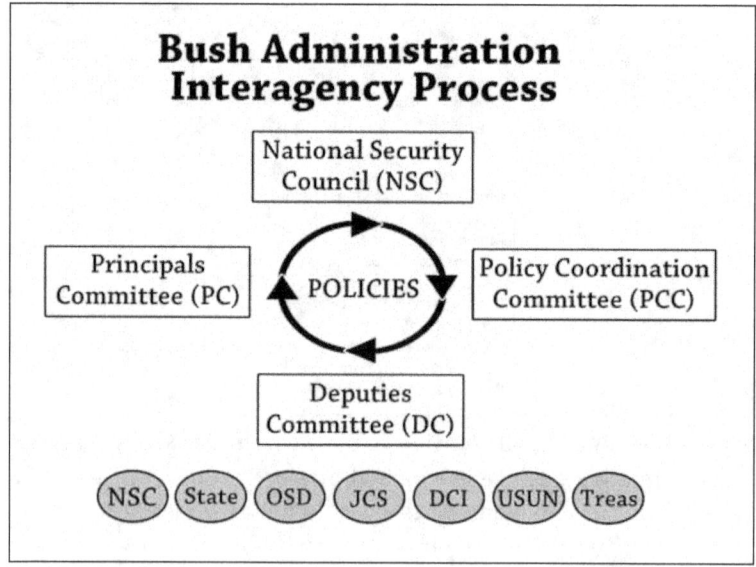

Bush Administration Interagency Process

Figure 1[21]

[strategic] interagency or "whole of government" apparatus starts at the highest level of the government's national security system.

With the operation in Iraq coming unhinged in 2005, in December of that year, President Bush published National Security Presidential Directive 44 (NSPD-44), which specifically directed the State Department to take the lead role in interagency coordination and established S/CRS.[25] NSPD-44 stated, "To achieve maximum effect, a focal point is needed (i) to coordinate and strengthen efforts of the United States Government to prepare, plan for, and conduct reconstruction and stabilization assistance and related activities in a range of situations that require the response capabilities of multiple United States Government entities and (ii) to harmonize such efforts with U.S. military plans and operations."

Specifically, the State Department and S/CRS are tasked with developing strategies for foreign assistance, planning and coordinating interagency response to foreign assistance needs, and compliance with the policies set forth in the 1961 Foreign Assistance Act.[26]

S/CRS's Core Mission "is to lead, coordinate and institutionalize U.S. Government civilian capacity to prevent or prepare for post-conflict situations, and to help stabilize and reconstruct societies in transition from conflict or civil strife, so they can reach a sustainable path toward peace, democracy and a market economy."[27] To accomplish this ambitious mission, S/CRS organizational plan calls for 250 active officers, 2,000 government officers on standby, an additional 2,000 in a reserve corps, and a requested [2010] budget of $323.3 million to start building capacity.[28] To give perspective, the Federal Air Marshal Service's 2010 budget request was $860.1 million—nearly 3 times the propose S/CRS budget request.[29]

That said, the creation S/CRS was a small step in the right direction. It was an attempt to organize the agency-to-agency coordination in order to effectively turn foreign policy into action. But despite its mandate under NSPD-44, it only has limited authority that is solely derived from the Secretary of State—it cannot compel other agencies or departments to commit personnel or resources to its efforts.[30] Thus, it has been slow to gain acceptance within the interagency community and has even met some resistance within the State Department.[31] S/CRS has also had difficulty getting traction in the field, missing valuable opportunities in Iraq and in Haiti after the January 2010 earthquake disaster. In Iraq, future reconstruction and development will be accomplished by embassy teams, and the disaster relief mission in Haiti was led by the USAID.[32] Without congressional support and legislative authority, other departments and agencies will continue to view S/CRS as an unfunded mandate without compulsory authority.[33]

Additionally, it can be argued that S/CRS duplicates many functions that have historically resided within USAID.[34] But unlike USAID, S/CRS falls squarely within the bureaucratic structure of the State Department. In contrast, USAID is a distinctly different and separate organization. It has a semi-autonomous relationship with the State and can be described as a partner rather than a subordinate.[35] Although a noble idea and a start in the right direction, this low cost approach is window dressing rather than a commitment to the whole-of-government concept. Naming the State Department as the lead for interagency operations may make sense considering its primary role in diplomacy and international relations. State's bureaucratic reality, however, makes this option must less viable. Even during the Marshall Plan in 1948, the conventional wisdom was that the State Department was not capable of administering the reconstruction of Europe; hence the Economic Cooperation Administration was created as a semi-autonomous executive agency.[36] USAID was established as an autonomous agency for much the same reason. In sum, although some changes have been made since 2001, the interagency process requires more far-reaching reform.

Interagency Process Reform

The post conflict stability and reconstruction operations in Iraq have sparked significant discussion in both academia and within government about reforming the national security apparatus as a whole, and the interagency process in particular. Since 2004, there has been a broad body of work done on this subject. Various studies have been conducted by notable think tanks, war colleges, the Congressional Research Service, and the Government Accountability Office and Congress itself (congressional hearings and committee investigations) with testimony from senior government officials and practitioners.

The studies' tenor is that coordination and collaboration between departments and agencies within the U.S. government needs to be improved. Although there is no clear consensus on what changes would enhance interagency cooperation, the scope of suggestions include clarifying roles and responsibilities, changing agency organizational structures and culture, integrating planning and execution, creating an over-arching interagency national security strategy, realigning distribution of resources, and providing congressional oversight. [37]

After a comprehensive review of the interagency process, one can reasonably conclude that interagency coordination is problematic but it is functional. Within the NSC, the Deputies Committee and the Interagency Policy Committee are capable of making timely policy decisions and managing the day-to-day coordination of interagency policy issues at the strategic level.[38] The process also appears to work at the tactical level with the practitioner in the field. The Joint Interagency Task Force (JIATF) South, the State Department's country teams, and the Provincial Reconstruction Teams serve as examples of measured success in the field.[39] However, it is important to note that the examples above took significant time to develop, mature, and produce positive results.[40]

The weakness within the interagency process is at the agency level, specifically among the domestic agencies.[41] At this level, between the strategic and tactical, the individual agencies are required to coordinate the details of resource allocation, funding, and roles and responsibilities in order to transform policy into action. Effective control of interagency operations fades away below the National Security Council and then reappears at the tactical level through ingenuity and force of personality on the ground. There is no coherent mechanism in the middle to consistently turn national security policy into effective actions in the field. It is here, in the middle, where interagency coordination and collaboration becomes difficult and can break down. [42] There is a natural tension and even reluctance among agencies to provide personnel and resources to foreign-service missions that lie outside the bounds of their core mission. Additionally, there is no government-wide protocol for deploying domestic agency personnel.[43] Each agency has its unique policies, regulations, and procedures that must be reconciled before agencies take action. Pre-deployment training, funding for temporary duty (TDY), and hazardous duty benefits all complicate coordination and collaboration. And although S/CRS provides pre-deployment training for partner agency personnel, there is no common doctrine among the various agencies to ensure unity of effort, unity of command, or clear lines of funding.[44] The problem lies in the middle, where the allocation and integration of resources must take place. Without an organization designed to coordinate and harmonize activities as well as marshal and direct resources, the interagency effort will be paralyzed by competing priorities.

Interagency reform that would bring a whole-of-government approach resulting in agile and responsive smart power requires several baseline conditions. First, whoever is responsible for interagency coordination must have authority that is commensurate with their mandate.[45] Second, there must be an established framework that clearly establishes a common overarching strategy, provides a unity of command, or at the very least unity of effort, through clear delineation of roles and responsibilities, providing an adequate funding scheme among the partnered agencies.[46] Third, there must be career incentives within the various domestic agencies that reward foreign interagency service. This will ensure the right people actively seek participation within the interagency foreign-service domain.[47] None of these conditions can happen without a congressional mandate, legislative authority, and congressional oversight.[48] Two viable options exist for interagency reform. One, a reconceptualized S/CRS or, two, a reinvigorated USAID.

To change S/CRS, policymakers could look to the Federal Emergency Management Agency (FEMA) as the best insight for interagency cooperation. After severe criticism following Hurricane Katrina, FEMA was transformed into an action oriented, operationalized agency.[49] The Stafford Act provided both the framework and the authority to effectively coordinate and harmonize the interagency effort.[50] S/CRS and FEMA share similar missions and mandates. They are both tasked to lead and coordinate interagency activities. For FEMA, the focus is on domestic hazards, so it is geared to marshal interagency capacities to protect against natural and man-made disasters at home.[51] S/CRS, on the other hand, is driven by foreign stability and reconstruction operations and aims to project the whole of government capacity to prevent conflict and/or assist nations that are recovering from conflict or civil strife. In both cases the goal is essentially the same: harmonize interagency collaboration in a unified effort.

The problem with S/CRS is that it falls under the weight of the State Department bureaucracy. S/CRS's authority is derived from, and limited by, the Secretary of State's authority. It is essentially an unfunded mandate without teeth or traction.[52] If this first course of interagency reform is chosen, S/CRS should be transformed into a semi-autonomous, self-contained, and fully funded organization. It must have Congressionally granted legal authority, an organizational framework, and operating process. Revamping S/CRS in this fashion is not without historical precedent.

As the Marshall Plan was built, debate emerged over who would administer the reconstruction and recovery effort in post-WWII Europe. The end result was the creation of the semi-autonomous Economic Cooperation Administration (ECA). The ECA led the European reconstruction and recovery effort by coordinating and directing various U.S. and coalition government agencies. The Marshall Plan and the ECA is perhaps the first and most meaningful projection of soft power in U.S. history.

The Foreign Assistance Act and the creation of the U.S. Agency for International Development (USAID) serve as other historical examples. On September 4, 1961, Congress reorganized and consolidated non-military U.S. foreign assistance programs into a single independent organization. In compliance with this legislation, President Kennedy established the U.S. Agency for International Development. USAID has since established a long history of implementing economic and technical assistance to foreign countries, projecting U.S. soft power in support of national interests.[53]

Despite these examples, it is unlikely that the U.S. Congress would create another large, semi-autonomous bureaucratic organization. Financial cost and essentially duplicating the bureaucracy that exists within USAID may not be practical. A viable compromise may be to replicate FEMA's model with legislation similar to the Stafford Act which established both the legal authority and administrative framework (Emergency Response Framework) for FEMA. This legislation "operationalized" FEMA and made it an effective and responsive interagency broker.[54] In this model, once an international crisis is identified by Presidential declaration, S/CRS's legal authorities would engage. The "Crisis Response Framework" would be activated and S/CRS would then have legal authority and funding to direct and compel partner agencies to support the assigned foreign assistance mission (see below). This assumes, of course, that the infrastructure and operational framework would already be established, and that a standing interagency reserve force (Civilian Response Corps) would be trained, organized, and equipped to deploy on short notice.

A second option is to reinforce and reform USAID, an organization with a long history of foreign assistance. USAID has an existing legacy, culture, and organizational structure that supports foreign assistance and development missions. It has well established and habitual relationships with both the Department of State and the Department of Defense, two critical partners in foreign affairs.[55] Recent history has demonstrated that USAID is the agency of choice, and perhaps the most capable of deploying rapidly to trouble spots. It has been active in Iraq, Afghanistan, and most recently in Haiti's earthquake recovery. USAID may be the "natural" answer to the interagency/foreign service question. It makes sense to reform and reinforce an existing institution,

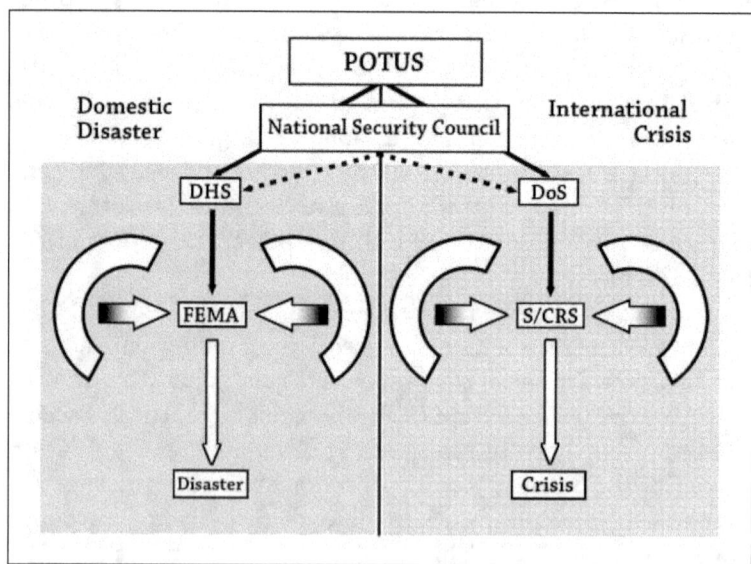

Figure 2

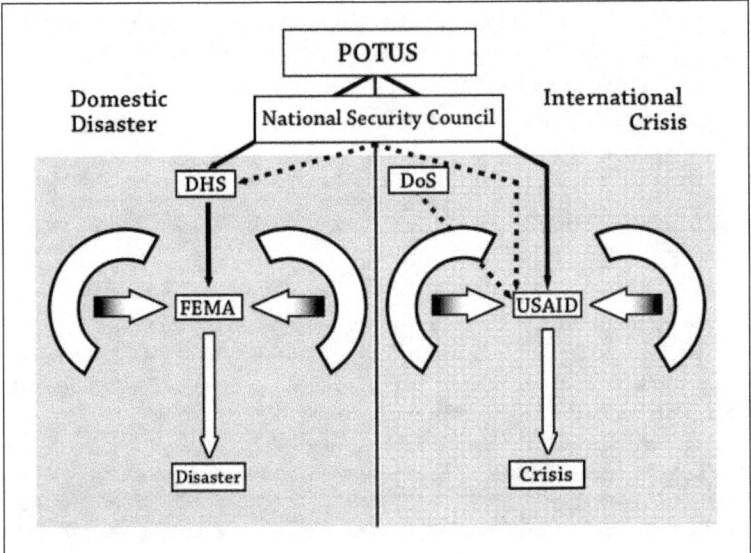

Figure 3

with all its organizational and bureaucratic trappings, rather than to create an additional and perhaps duplicate bureaucracy from scratch. Not only would bolstering USAID be less complicated and more cost effective, it would also take less time.

However, one can glean from history that increasing USAID's capacity and adding to its responsibilities, even in the margins, will meet with resistance. It stands to reason that if USAID is tasked with coordinating the interagency enterprise abroad, it will still need enhanced legislative authority, increased funding and an operational framework based in legislation analogous to the FEMA model (see above).

In any case, whatever organization is made responsible for interagency coordination, there must be significant reform to the national security and national strategy process. As outlined in the 2005 CSIS report, *Beyond Goldwater-Nichols: U.S. Government and Defense Reform for a New Strategic Era*, the entire national security framework is in need of overhaul. Creating a new statutory framework the spans the entire government will greatly facilitate cooperation. This framework should include measures that address: strategic and operational planning across the entire government, agency roles and responsibilities with regard to national security, creating an overarching national security strategy, and providing oversight through a government-wide National Security Quadrennial Review. These radical steps will require an act of Congress. Given the national security stakes, it is past time for Congress to engage.

Notes

[1]House Committee on Armed Services, *Improving Interagency Coordination for the Global War on Terror,* 109th Cong., 2nd sess., April 4, 2006, (Washington DC: GPO, 2007), 61. Also available at: http://frwebgate.access.gpo.gov/cgi-bin/get-doc.cgi?dbname=109_house_hearings&docid=f:32971.pdf.

[2]U.S. Government Accountability Office, *Interagency Collaboration: Key Issues from Congressional Oversight of National Security Strategies, Organizations, Workforce, and Information Sharing,* September 2009, Congressional Committees, (Washington DC: GAO, 2009), 4. Also available online at: http://www.gao.gov/new.items/d09904sp.pdf.

[3]Jay Bendes (Principal Interagency Management Officer, Office of the Coordinator for Reconstruction and Stabilization), interviewed by the author, March 16, 2010.

[4]Ibid.

[5]Ibid.

[6]Center for Strategic and International Studies, *Beyond Goldwater-Nichols: U.S. Government and Defense Reform for a New Strategic Era* (Washington D.C: July 2005), 6-21.

[7]Bendes, interview, March 16, 2010.

[8]Ibid.

[9]Dale Andrade and James H. Willbanks, "CORDS/Phoenix: Counterinsurgency Lessons from Vietnam for the Future," *Military Review,* March-April 2006, http://www.cgsc.edu/carl/resources/willbanks.pdf (March 12, 2010).

[10]Jim Willbanks, January 9, 2009 (11:00 a.m.), "CGSC History Department: FM 3-07 and CORDS," Combined Arms Center Blog Library, http://usacac.army.mil/BLOG/blogs/hist/archive/2009/01/09/fm-3-07-and-cords.aspx (March 12, 2010).

[11]Ron Capps, "What's the Story on Militarization?" *Frontlines,* November 2009, http://www.usaid.gov/press/frontlines/fl_nov09/p02_capps091104.html (March 12, 2010).

[12]*Congressional Reports: H.rpt.109-377- A Failure of Initiative: Final Report of the Select Bipartisan Committee to Investigate the Preparation for and Response to Hurricane Katrina,* March 31, 2008, http://www.gpoaccess.gov/serialset/creports/katrina.html (March 12, 2010).

[13]U.S. House of Representatives, Committee on Armed Services. Subcommittee on Oversight & Investigations, *Agency Stovepipes vs. Strategic Agility: Lessons We*

Need to Learn from Provincial Reconstruction Teams in Iraq and Afghanistan, 13-16, http://armedservises.house.gov/pdfs/Reports/PRT_Report.pdf (March 12, 2010).

[14]"Other Agencies on Mission's 'Country Team,'" *U.S. Diplomacy: An Online Exploration of Diplomatic History and Foreign Affairs*, U.S. Diplomacy, http://www.usdiplomacy.org/state/abroad/countryteam.php.

[15]George W. Bush, *National Security Presidential Directive/NSPD- 44* (Washington DC: The White House, December 7, 2005), http://www.fas.org/irp/offdocs /nspd/nspd-44.html.

[16]*National Security Act of 1947*, U.S. Code 50 (1947), §401, http://intelligence .senate.gov/nsaact1947.pdf (March 12, 2010).

[17]Barack Obama, *Presidential Policy Directive-1*, "Organization of the National Security Council System" (Washington DC: The White House, February 13, 2009), http://www.fas.org/irp/offdocs/ppd/ppd-1.pdf (March 12, 2010).

[18]Chairman of the Joint Chiefs of Staff, *Joint Publication 3-08: Interagency, Intergovernmental Organization, and Nongovernmental Organization Coordination During Joint Operations Vol I*, (Washington DC: GPO, March 17, 2006), II-4.

[19]Ibid., x

[20]Ibid.

[21]Gabriel Marcella, "National Security and the Interagency Process," *Guide to National Security Policy and Strategy, 2nd Edition*, J. Boone Bartholomees, Jr., ed., http://faculty.nps.edu/dl/PFP/pages/04_process.html (March 12, 2010).

[22]Richard Doyle, "Developing Security Strategy: The U.S. Approach," *Office of Continuous Learning at the Naval Postgraduate School*, http://faculty.nps .edu/dl/PFP/pages/04_process.html.

[23]JCS, *Joint Publication 3-08*, x.

[24]*Obama, Directive-1.*

[25]Bush, *National Security.*

[26]Ibid.

[27]"About Us," *U.S. Department of State*, http://www.state.gov/s/crs/about /index .htm.

[28]"Presidential FY 2010 Budget Request for the Civilian Stabilization Initiative," *U.S. Department of State*, http://www.crs.state.gov/index.cfm?fuseaction=public.display&shortcut=4QJW (March 12, 2010).

[29]U.S. Government Accountability Office, *Federal Air Marshal Service: Actions Taken to Fulfill Core Mission and Address Workforce Issue*, testimony, July 23, 2009, before the U.S. House, Subcommittee on Management, Investigations, and Oversight, Committee on Homeland Security, http://www.gao.gov/htext /d09903t.html (March 12, 2010).

[30]Bendes, interview, March 16, 2010.

[31]Ibid.

[32]Jonathan Benton (Principal Deputy Coordinator, Office of the Coordinator for Reconstruction and Stabilization), interviewed by the author, March 12, 2010.

[33]Bendes, interview, March 16, 2010.

[34]Ibid.

[35]U.S. Department of State and U.S. Agency for International Development,

Strategic Plan: Fiscal Years 2007-2012, U.S. Agency for International Development, May 7, 2007, http://www.state.gov/documents/organization/86291.pdf, 4-7.

[36]Charles M. Dobbs, *Economic Cooperation Act of 1948 (Marshall Plan),* http://www.encyclopedia.com/doc/ 1G2-3407400075.html (March 12, 2010).

[37]Congressional Research Service, *Organizing the U.S. Government for National Security: Overview of the Interagency Reform Debate,* December 16, 2008, http://fpc.state.gov/documents/organization/104695.pdf, 3.

[38]Benton, interview, March 12, 2010.

[39]Ibid.

[40]Ibid.

[41]Bendes, interview, March 16, 2010.

[42]Ibid.

[43]Benton, interview, March 12, 2010.

[44]Ibid.

[45]Ibid.

[46]Ibid.

[47]Center for Strategic and International Studies (CSIS), *Beyond Goldwater-Nichols,* 59.

[48]Ibid., 58-59.

[49]GPO, *A Failure of Initiative.*

[50]*Robert T. Stafford Disaster Relief and Emergency Assistance Act,* U.S. Code 42 (1974), §5121.

[51]Visit to Federal Management Agency, Marine Corps War College, Washington DC, February 2010.

[52]Bendes, interview, March 16, 2010.

[53]"USAID: History," *U.S. Agency for International Development,* April 3, 2009, http://www.usaid.gov/about_usaid/usaidhist.html.

[54]*Relief and Emergency Assistance Act,* U.S. Code 42.

[55]Bendes, interview, March 16, 2010.

Establishing U.S. Stability Operations Command: An Organization for the Critical National Security Missions of the 21st Century

by Doug M. Hammer

ABSTRACT

The United States' investment, in both blood and treasure, toward its national security has garnered a world in which it has no peer competitor in the traditional warfare arena. As a result, those who wish to threaten U.S. security have been forced to evolve their methods and now engage through indirect and unconventional means using failed or failing states as their base. Consequently, modern conflicts are no longer resolved with quick and decisive victories on the battlefield but rather with the stabilization of vulnerable states.

To greatly simplify U.S. national defense strategy of the past, when national security relied upon victory of the battlefield, defense equated to traditional warfare. Given the success of that strategy and evolution of irregular warfare, defense now equates to stability operations. This shift in strategy has been codified in both our national strategic framework documents as well as in Department of Defense policy. Department of Defense Directive (DODD) 3005.05, *Stability Operations*, states, "stability operations are a core U.S. military mission that the DOD shall be prepared to conduct with proficiency equivalent to combat operations." While U.S. national strategy has shifted to compensate for the changing threat, its supporting processes and organizational structures are still hindered by the historic mindset of defense. The good news is that the very legal basis of the U.S.

armed services, Title 10 of the U.S. Code, provides not only the opportunity but the requirement to periodically review national security threats and adjust the defense framework accordingly. Additionally, history has provided the United States with case studies where the threat and nature of conflict has shifted.

With the advent of nuclear weapons, deterrence rather than traditional combat operations became a major component of U.S. national security. As a result the U.S. national security leadership used the flexibility provided in Title 10, United States Code to establish a functional combatant command to focus on deterrence and thus U.S. Strategic Command was born. Once again the United States finds itself faced with a new threat and once again it must restructure its organizational framework to meet the threat. The establishment of U.S. Stability Operations Command will not only posture the military to execute current national security policy and strategy but also provide a structure to effectively leverage the capabilities of the interagency team.

ORGANIZING FOR 21ST CENTURY SECURITY THREATS AND OPPORTUNITIES

To better organize for critical national security missions of the 21st century and successfully integrate interagency stabilization and reconstruction related activities, the Department of Defense (DOD) should establish a single, functional combatant command for stability operations. U.S. Stability Operations Command would not only improve DOD's ability to plan, prepare for, and execute stability operations, but would also provide the military's organizational framework for all members of the interagency involved in this vital mission. With DOD's planning and logistics capabilities as the backbone of U.S. Stability Operations Command, other resource challenged members of the interagency team could focus their limited capacity on providing planning and operational expertise to whole-of-government operations with a single military point of contact.

The United States has determined that weak and failing states pose significant threats to its national security and is committed to helping countries prevent or emerge from conflict. In the face of these threats, President Bush issued National Security Presidential Directive 44, *Management of Interagency Efforts Con-*

cerning Reconstruction and Stabilization, recognizing that the United States has a significant stake in enhancing its capacity to stabilize and reconstruct countries or regions. In support of NSPD-44, the Secretary of Defense issued Department of Defense Directive (DODD) 3000.05, *Military Support for Stability, Security, Transition, and Reconstruction Operations* that provided policy and assigned responsibility for planning, preparing for, and executing stability operations. More importantly, DODD 3000.05 defined stability operations as a core military mission on par with combat operations.

Since the signing of NSPD-44 in December 2005, a number of Departmental and Congressional level studies and reports have concluded that the greatest challenge to the U.S. Government's (USG's) ability to conduct stability operations is the lack of an integrated planning capability and the capacity of civilian agencies with which the military must partner to achieve success. While the DOD can fill some of these gaps in civilian capacity in the short-term, strategic success will only be possible with a robust architecture for unified civil-military action. The continuing challenge facing interagency leadership has become how to best address the capacity, planning, and organizational framework shortfalls within the currently flawed architecture. Fortunately, the legal basis of the military provides national leaders the ability to restructure commands and forces as required to meet changes within the strategic environment.

Title 10, U.S. Code, requires that the Chairman of the Joint Chiefs of Staff (CJCS) review combatant commands' missions and responsibilities within the military every two years and recommend to the President, through the Secretary of Defense, any changes that may be necessary. The results of this review are published in the form of the Unified Command Plan (UCP). An examination of the UCP history illustrates that past national leaders have used this requirement, although grudgingly at times, to adjust roles and missions as threats to U.S. national security have evolved. In response to the current operating environment, the most recent UCP, signed by President Bush in December 2008, assigned all combatant commanders responsibility for planning and conducting military support to stability operations. While this change has the potential to improve the military's ability to conduct stability operations, it does little to address the fundamental challenge of interagency synchronization because other U.S. government agencies simply do not have the capacity to provide expertise to each of our combatant commands. This chapter seeks to make the case for creating a U.S. Stability Operations Command by, first, laying out the strategic context. Then, the current constructs and capabilities to address the operating environment will be addressed, followed by an analysis of the proposal for a U.S. Stability Operations Command. The chapter ends by identifying the way forward.

STRATEGIC CONTEXT FOR STABILITY OPERATIONS

To fully comprehend the challenges associated with conducting successful stability operations, it is necessary to examine the strategic context. This examination starts by reviewing the transformation of warfare and defining the concept of stability operations along with its primary missions, tasks, and activities; by assessing the U.S. experience with stability operations in order to draw any conclusions which can be applied to future operations; and by reviewing the current national strategy for conducting stability operations in the form of U.S. policy and doctrine. Only by understanding this strategic context can leaders devise an effective architecture for conducting stability operations in support of national interests.

Traditional warfare is characterized as a confrontation between nation-states or coalitions/alliances of nation-states. This confrontation typically involves force-on-force military combat operations in which adversaries employ a variety of conventional military capabilities against each other.[1] Past U.S. investment, in both blood and treasure, toward its national security has resulted in a world which it currently has no peer competitor in the traditional warfare arena. As a result, those who wish to threaten U.S. security have been forced to transform their methods and engage through irregular means. The environment of irregular warfare (IW) is marked by a violent struggle among state and non-state actors for legitimacy and influence over the relevant population. IW favors indirect and asymmetric approaches in order to erode an adversary's power, influence, and will. In IW, a less powerful adversary seeks to disrupt or negate the military capabilities and advantages of a more powerful, conventionally armed military force. IW typically manifests itself as one or a combination of several possible forms, including insurgency, terrorism, disinformation, propaganda, or organized criminal activity. An adversary will vary the form of IW according to its capabilities and objectives.

What makes IW "irregular" is the focus of its operations, a relevant population, and its strategic purpose, to gain or maintain control or influence over, and the support of, that relevant population through political, psychological, and economic methods. Warfare that has the population as its operational focus requires a different mindset and different capabilities than warfare that focuses on defeating an adversary militarily.[2] When engaged in IW, an U.S. response should vary according to established objectives along with the specific type(s) of operation(s) required.

An effective strategy in countering IW is to ensure potential adversaries cannot find a host state in which to conduct its operations. Fragile states provide the fuel for adversaries to spread its fire. Stabilizing these fragile states starves the flame of its fuel, leaving it to die out. Consequently, the majority of modern conflicts are no longer resolved with quick and decisive victories on the battlefield, but rather with the stabilization of vulnerable states.

Joint Publication (JP) 3.07, defines stability operations as, "encompassing various military missions, tasks, and activities conducted outside the United States in coordination with other instruments of national power to maintain or reestablish a safe and secure environment, provide essential governmental services, emergency infrastructure reconstruction, and humanitarian relief."[3] An examination of this definition provides insight into the structures and planning required to execute the various activities associated with stability operations.

The phrase "encompassing various military missions, tasks, and activities" indicates that stability operations are broad in scope and not limited to traditional military activities. Likewise, actions to plan and prepare for stability operations are different from those of conventional combat operations. Including the phrase "conducted . . . in coordination with other instruments of national power" makes it clear that stability operations are part of a larger interagency effort which implies the need for a whole of government, integrated planning capability. Finally, the JP 3-07 definition lists four primary activities within stability operations: (1) maintaining/reestablishing a safe and secure environment, (2) providing essential government services, (3) providing emergency infrastructure, and (4) providing humanitarian relief. Although this definition may seem straightforward, it becomes complex when being executed by dissimilar organizations across initial response, transformational, and long-term sustainment activities.[4] Designing a strategy to determine which organization executes which tasks, and at what time, is largely determined by the security level of the environment in which stability operations are conducted. In a non-permissive environment, the military will be the primary, if not sole, executor of stability operations, at least in the field on the ground. Once the task of maintaining a safe and secure environment is accomplished, the major factor in determining a strategy becomes the organizational core competencies of those involved in the stability operation. As suggested by this expanded definition, stability operations activities may be executed solely by the military or in cooperation with Department of State (DOS), non-governmental organizations (NGOs), or host nation institutions.

Although defining stability operations and understanding its primary activities are important steps to addressing shortfalls in the current execution strategy, assessing the U.S. experience with stability operations provides an opportunity to draw conclusions that can be applied to a future organizational framework, capacity, and planning shortfalls. In the more than two centuries since its existence, U.S. forces have fought eleven wars that were conventional in nature. Of those conflicts, four were total wars (War of Independence, Civil War, and World Wars I and II), in which the nation's existence or its way of life was considered to be at stake, and in which few restrictions were placed on the weapons employed or on the targets attacked in the military's efforts to defeat the enemy. The remaining seven wars (War of 1812, Mexican War, Spanish-American War, Korean and Vietnam wars, and two Gulf wars) were limited in that an imminent threat to the country's survival or way of life was not apparent, thereby allowing U.S. policy makers to accept or set limitations on the objectives, scope, and/or conduct of hostilities. Throughout its history, the U.S. military has focused the bulk of its attention on fighting, or preparing to fight, these kinds of conventional wars, with circumstances dictating whether any given conflict would be total or limited.[5]

As the Cold War ended, the world became more complex and unstable as ethnic, religious, tribal, and other local and regional conflicts, repressed, ignored, or sponsored by the superpowers' regional ambitions during the Cold War, would become more prominent and increasingly disruptive. In the decade of the 1990s, local conflicts emerged or reemerged on virtually every continent, and as the U.S. military found itself gainfully employed and deployed throughout the world. Many of these efforts continued into the new century, and incursions into Afghanistan and Iraq revealed an increasing trend throughout the world—the collapse of established governments, the rise of international criminal and terrorist networks, and a seemingly endless array of humanitarian crises. The global implications of such destabilizing forces have proved staggering. If the country's armed forces have fought fewer than a dozen major conventional wars in over two centuries, they have, during that same period, engaged in several hundred military undertakings that would today be characterized as stability operations.[6] Therefore, contrary to widely accepted beliefs, U.S. military history is dominated by stability operations, interrupted by distinct instances of major combat. With such a large number of case studies in the past, it is prudent to study them in order to derive lessons that can be applied to the current and future strategy of stability operations.

An historic assessment of U.S. stability operations over a 207-year period was published in *The U.S. Military's Experience in Stability Operations, 1798-2005.* Specific conclusions drawn from that assessment that can be applied to future stability operations included the following: (1) stability operations will be conducted in a joint, interagency, and multinational environment; (2) the U.S. military will play a critical role in stability operations; (3) the U.S. military will bear some significant responsibility for planning in the pre-execution phase of stability operations; and (4) the U.S. military must be capable of conducting stability operations simultaneously with other military operations.[7] These conclusions were validated by Secretary of Defense Gates: "We know that at least in the early phases of any conflict, contingency, or natural disaster, the U.S. military—as has been the case throughout our history—will be responsible for security, reconstruction, and providing basic sustenance and public services."[8] Based upon these historical conclusions, it is clear that despite any desire or design to the contrary, the military must remain a principal partner in conducting, and therefore planning, stability operations. As the nation's leaders have come to terms with this realization, U.S. strategy for conducting stability operations has and must continue to evolve. The U.S. National Security Strategy is based on a distinct internationalist tone that reflects the interests and values of the country. It clearly aims to make the world a safer place where a community of nations lives in relative peace. To that end, the National Security Strategy and subordinate supporting strategies, focus on progress that promotes political and economic freedom, peaceful relations with other nations, and universal respect for human dignity.

The body of security strategy that shapes the conduct of stability operations includes the National Security Strategy (NSS), the National Defense Strategy (NDS), and the National Military Strategy (NMS). Together with other supporting national policy, strategy provides the broad direction necessary to conduct operations to support national interests. (See figure 1.)

The National Security Strategy (NSS)[9] outlines the President's vision for enduring security for the American people in a volatile, uncertain, and complex strategic environment. It sets a course for statecraft, providing the broad national strategy for applying the instruments of national power to further U.S. interests globally. History has shown that fragile states tend to attract destabilizing forces, which poses a national security challenge unforeseen even a decade ago, yet central to today's strategic environment. While the concept of fragile states is not new, the need for a strategy to provide a stabilizing influence is more critical than ever. At the heart of this strategy is the U.S. approach to stability operations: to help create a world of well-governed states that can meet the needs of their citizens and conduct themselves responsibly. This challenge is at the core of the current NSS.

Signed by President Obama in May 2010, the most recent

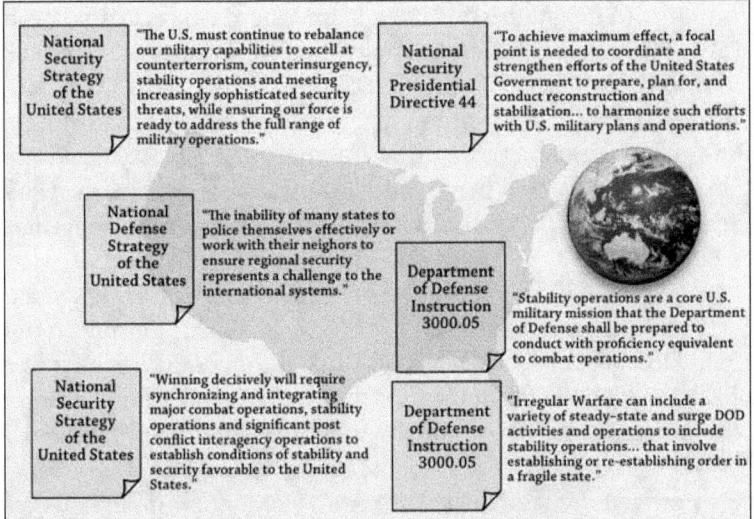

Figure 1: Stability operations strategy and policy references[10]

NSS outlines a strategy that includes an international order advanced by U.S. leadership, which promotes peace, security, and opportunity through stronger cooperation to meet global challenges. Implementing this agenda will not be easy. To succeed, the United States must balance and integrate all elements of national power and update its national security capacity for the 21st century. Furthermore, the United States must maintain its military's conventional superiority, while enhancing its capacity to defeat asymmetric threats. Specifically, the United States must continue to rebalance its military capabilities to excel at counterterrorism, counterinsurgency, and stability operations; meet increasingly sophisticated security threats; and ensure U.S. forces are ready to address the full range of military operations—and they must do all of this simultaneously. Although military participation in stability operations within a non-permissive environment may be obvious, what is not as clear is that continued involvement across the full spectrum of conflict is necessary because the transitions between pre-conflict, conflict, and post-conflict are not always apparent or linear.

Reinforcing the direction of the NSS, the National Defense Strategy[11] emphasizes national security threats posed by fragile states' inability to police themselves, or to work in cooperation with neighbor states to ensure long-term security. These states often undermine regional stability, threatening broader U.S. interests. The most recent NDS, published in June 2008, recognizes the need for building partner capacity in these states. Built on the understanding that U.S. national security is closely tied to security within the broader international system, the NDS focuses on using programs to build partnerships that strengthen the host nation's ability to confront security challenges.

The NDS also recognizes the need to foster interagency coordination and integration in these efforts. Such efforts draw a vital link between the DOD and DOS in the conduct of stability operations. The NDS emphasizes the need to establish conditions of enduring security to support stability operations that allows the other instruments of national power to conduct their operations as well. Unless the security environment supports using civilian agencies and organizations, military forces must be prepared to perform those nonmilitary tasks normally the responsibility of others. Thus, the NDS clearly establishes the intent of the Secretary of Defense to focus efforts on tasks directly associated with establishing favorable long-term security conditions.

Prepared by the Chairman of the Joint Chiefs of Staff, the National Military Strategy[12] is consistent with the NSS and NDS. It specifies the ends, ways, and means necessary to ensure national security and to pursue national interests at home and abroad. It also describes and analyzes the strategic environment as it affects military operations, and identifies the most significant threats in that environment. The most recent NMS, published in March 2005, stresses interagency integration, emphasizing the role of interagency partners and NGOs in achieving lasting success in stability operations. It establishes the requirement for the joint force to retain the capability to conduct full spectrum operations, combining offensive, defensive, and stability tasks simultaneously and to seamlessly transition between them. Finally, it highlights the need to integrate conflict termination measures with other instruments of national power, ensuring unity of effort toward national objectives.

In 2005, President Bush signed National Security Presidential Directive 44 (NSPD-44).[13] NSPD-44 outlined the President's vision for promoting security through improved coordination, planning, and implementation of reconstruction and stabilization assistance. This policy was the Bush administration's first attempt at defining national policy for interagency integration. In addition, NSPD-44 formally acknowledged that the stability of foreign states serves the broader national interests and recognized stability operations as a necessary capability.

NSPD-44 outlines the need for coordinated U.S. efforts to achieve maximum effect within stability operations. Specifically, it asserts a focal point is required to coordinate and strengthen efforts of the USG in preparation, planning, and conducting reconstruction and stabilization assistance activities in a range of situations that require the response capabilities of multiple USG entities. Furthermore, NSPD-44 calls for harmonizing other USG stabilization efforts with U.S. military plans and operations. To accomplish this goal, NSPD-44 assigns lead agency responsibility to the DOS, directing the Secretary of State to coordinate and lead integrated USG efforts and activities. It also mandates that DOS coordinate with the DOD to ensure the integration and synchronization of any planned or ongoing military operations across the spectrum of conflict. Also in 2005, the Secretary of Defense signed DODD 3000.05, *Military Support for Stability, Security, Transition, and Reconstruction (SSTR) Operations*[14] providing the military force with definitive guidance to conduct stability operations, giving it the same level of importance as combat operations. In September 2009, the Secretary of Defense approved DODD 3000.05, *Stability Operations* that reissues DODD 3000.05 as an instruction and assigns responsibility for planning, preparing for, and executing stability operations.

DODI 3000.05 reemphasized that stability operations are a core U.S. military mission that the DOD shall be prepared to conduct with proficiency equivalent to combat operations. Specifically, it stated DOD shall be prepared to: (1) conduct stability operations activities throughout all phases of conflict and across the range of military operations, including in combat and non-combat environments; (2) support stability operations activities led by other USG departments or agencies, foreign governments and security forces, or international governmental organizations; and (3) lead stability operations activities until such time as it is feasible to transition lead responsibility to other USG agencies, foreign governments and security forces, or international governmental organizations. In such circumstances, DOD will operate within USG and international structures for managing civil-military operations, and will seek to enable the utilization of the appropriate civilian capabilities.

In addition to defining what actions various DOD components will accomplish, DODI 3000.05 recognizes that integrated civilian and military efforts are essential to the conduct of successful stability operations. In support of that belief, it requires that DOD components will collaborate with and support other USG agencies, NGOs, and private sector firms to plan, prepare for, and conduct stability operations. Furthermore, it charged DOD to support the development, implementation, and operations of civil-military teams and related efforts aimed at unity of effort in executing reconstruction and stabilization efforts, as well as building indigenous capacity for such tasks. Finally, DODI 3000.05 charged DOD to integrate stability operations-related concepts across doctrine, organization, training, and applicable exercises, strategies, and plans.

NSPD-44 requires the Secretaries of State and Defense to integrate stabilization and reconstruction contingency plans with military contingency plans and develop a general framework for fully coordinating stabilization and reconstruction activities and military operations at all levels. This charge makes it clear that the two primary USG departments involved in executing stability operations are the DOS and the DOD. How these two departments interact in executing NSPD-44 is dependent upon their organizational structures as well as the roles and responsibilities assigned within each.

CURRENT CONSTRUCTS AND CAPABILITIES FOR STABILITY OPERATIONS

To assist the Secretary of State, NSPD-44 called on an interagency office within the DOS specifically created to enhance the nation's institutional capacity to respond to crises involving fragile states. Based on an April 2004 decision of the National Security Council principals committee, former Secretary of State Colin Powell created the Office of the Coordinator for Reconstruction and Stabilization (S/CRS) in July 2004. S/CRS was established to lead, coordinate, and institutionalize the USG civilian capacity for reconstruction and stabilization and conflict transformation. It is designed to create mechanisms, tools, and processes to help reconstruct and stabilize societies in countries at risk of, in, or in transition from violent conflict or civil strife so that they can reach a sustainable path toward peace, democracy, and a market economy.[15] S/CRS is the first USG entity specifically created to address stability operations.

To establish a stable and lasting peace based on the fundamentals of conflict transformation, stability operations capitalize on coordination, cooperation, integration, and synchronization among military and nonmilitary organizations. To that end, S/CRS has developed three distinct capabilities that can be customized in scale and scope. These capabilities include the Interagency Management System (IMS), the whole of government planning framework, and the Civilian Response Corps (CRC).

The IMS is a management structure designed to assist policymakers, chiefs of mission, and military commanders who manage complex reconstruction and stabilization activities. This structure assists them by ensuring coordination among all USG stakeholders at the strategic, operational, and tactical levels. The whole-of-government planning framework facilitates assessment and planning for complex crises that require significant and complex security, reconstruction, governance, and economic efforts utilizing all instruments of national power. The CRC stabilization initiative provides a standing civilian response capability with the training, equipment, and resources necessary for successful planning and the conduct of operations in the field.

In addition to the reconstruction and stabilization structure within S/CRS, the Secretary of State also has the U.S. Agency for International Development (USAID) as a leading organization for stability operations. USAID is the first U.S. foreign assistance organization whose primary emphasis is long-range economic and social development assistance efforts. With respect to stability operations, USAID's role is characterized as management and oversight. It actually delivers virtually all of its development assistance through implementing partners—frequently NGOs whom USAID either hires as contractors to accomplish specific tasks or funds through cooperative agreements. NSPD-44 makes it clear that DOD has a major role to play within the whole-of-government stability operations strategy. In response, DOD established policy and a framework that organizes its roles and responsibilities for stability operations. The defining policy is DODI 3000.05, and the three main organizational levels include the Office of the Secretary of Defense (OSD), Joint Chiefs of Staff (JCS), and Combatant Commands (COCOMs).

The primary function of OSD is the formulation of policy for DOD, to include stability operations policy. Within OSD, the Assistant Secretary of Defense for Special Operations and Low-Intensity Conflict and Interdependent Capabilities (ASD(SO/LIC&IC)) serves as the principal civilian advisor for stability operations, provides policy oversight to ensure that DOD maintains the capability and capacity to conduct stability operations activities, and ensures those capabilities are compatible with those of other USG agencies and partners. The Chairman of the JCS serves as the principal military advisor to the Secretary of Defense for stability operations and, in coordination with the CO-COMs, establishes priorities for the development of stability operations capabilities for the U.S. military. The Joint Staff J5 Global Strategic Partnerships/Stability Operations Division works closely with OSD to oversee DODI 3000.05 implementation.

As specified in the December 2008 Unified Command Plan (UCP), there are ten COCOMs; six have geographic responsibilities and four have functional responsibilities[16] with USSOCOM being unique in that it performs certain Service-like functions.[17] Each geographic COCOM is responsible to plan for and conduct military support to stability operations, while each functional COCOM is responsible for supporting the geographical COCOMs in planning efforts.[18] DOD provides strategic guidance on how to accomplish this planning through the Guidance for Employment of the Force (GEF). The GEF requires each geographic COCOM to develop campaign plans in support of their theater strategies. While COCOMs are given latitude in how these campaign plans can be constructed, they are expected to include a comprehensive integration of steady-state activities (security cooperation) with shaping activities (military and interagency) performed to assure or solidify relationships with friends or allies.

A critical element to this strategy-centric approach to planning is the forcing mechanism to synchronize global campaign plans, accomplished by functional COCOMs, with theater campaign plans. As the title implies, global campaign plans likely impact multiple theaters; therefore, geographic COCOMs must develop subordinate plans in support of the global campaign plans. These subordinate plans are then embedded in the geographic COMCOMs' theater campaign plan.[19] The 2008 Unified Command Plan calls for ten of these global campaign plans to include: Global Operations Against Terrorist Networks (USSOCOM); Homeland Defense; Defense Support to Civil Authorities; Global Pandemic Influenza; (USNORTHCOM), Strategic Deterrence; Space Operations; Information Operations; Global Strike; Intelligence, Surveillance, and Reconnaissance; and Combating Weapons of Mass Destruction (USSTRATCOM).[20]

To accomplish the integration of global and theater campaign plans, each COCOM is responsible for designating a Joint Force Coordinating Authority for stability operations with the authority to identify stability operations requirements, and incorporating stability operations activities and concepts into training, exercises, experimentation, and planning, including intelligence campaign and support planning. COCOMs also are charged with aligning their strategies and plans with complementary stability operations-related capabilities, strategies, and plans of other USG agencies, foreign government and security forces, and the private sector. Furthermore, COCOMs identify stability operations-related capability, capacity, or compatibility shortfalls, as well as gather lessons learned from stability operations and disseminate them to the DOD Components and USG agencies.[21]

To provide for the COCOMs need for greater coordination and integrated operations with its mission partners, DOD approved the concept of Joint and Interagency Coordination Groups (JIACG) to improve interagency cooperation and improve operational effectiveness. JIACGs are tailored to meet the requirements and challenges of each COCOM's area of operation, and may include representatives from a wide range of USG agencies, the intelligence community, as well as NGOs. The JIACG concept seeks to establish operational connections between civilian and military departments, agencies, and services to improve planning and coordination within the government.

The JIACG is a multi-functional advisory element that

represents civilian departments and agencies to facilitate information sharing across the interagency community. It provides regular, timely, and collaborative day-to-day working relationships between civilian and military operational planners. Members participate in deliberate, crisis, and transition planning, and provide links back to their parent civilian agencies to help synchronize operations with the efforts of civilian USG agencies and departments. JIACGs are designed to strengthen USG interagency operational planning, increase effectiveness through more integrated operational planning and tactical execution between civilian and military agencies, and coordinate options involving all elements of national power to key decision-makers.[22]

Despite all of these structures, interagency coordination for stability operations remains ineffective at best and ineffectual at worst. Both DOS and DOD have established organizational frameworks to implement NSPD-44 requirements for stability operations, yet both internal and independent reviews of the USG's ability to conduct stability operations continue to reveal these frameworks are not effective in planning and executing stability operations.

A plethora of studies on stability operations have come out in the last decade.[23] The conclusions drawn by these various studies and reports have centered on its two main players' inability to plan and prepare for stability operations. As the USG's lead for stability operations, the DOS has failed to implement an effective interagency planning system. Furthermore, DOS lacks adequate resources and influence to effectively lead the interagency charge toward stability operations. Recognizing this fact, DOD has been more than willing to step forward and tap into its extensive expertise in crisis and deliberate planning to lead the USG charge. However, a lack of civilian department and interagency capacity leads to non-DOD organizations having a limited capacity to participate in DOD's full range of planning activities at each COCOM. Also, without a clear executive agent and advocate within DOD, it has failed to incorporate lessons learned into the planning process and has not adequately adjusted the balance between better training for stability operations and for traditional combat operations.

The good news is DOD identified one of the nation's key strategic issues: "while [DOD] has the capability and capacity to fulfill most stability operations requirements in the short term, long-term strategic success still requires a robust architecture with appropriate capacity for integrated civil-military action and substantially more resources devoted to increasing the operational and expeditionary capacity of civilian USG departments and agencies."[24] What DOD has yet to realize is the limited effectiveness of its own current structure. No matter what level of civilian capacity exists (or does not exist), DOD requires an organizational structure that has the power and responsibility on behalf of the U.S. military for stability operations.

THE FUNCTIONAL COMBATANT COMMAND SOLUTION

According to most of the research, the USG's ability to plan and conduct stability operations still requires changes within the interagency, specifically DOS and DOD. Fortunately, examination of history can provide a solution as this is not the first time that a shift in the national security environment has resulted in the need for transformation within DOD. In fact, the very legal basis for our military, Title 10 USC, not only permits periodic reviews of the U.S. military organizational structure viewed against current threats, it makes such reviews mandatory.[25]

In order to protect U.S. national security interests, the military must be an efficient team of land, naval, and air forces. To this end, the President establishes unified commands to bring about unity of effort among the services. The Unified Command Plan (UCP) establishes COCOMs, identifies geographic areas of responsibility, assigns primary tasks, defines authority of the commanders, and gives guidance on the exercise of combatant command.

Unified Combatant Commands (or simply combatant commands) were first described in the National Security Act of 1947 and the statutory definition has not changed since that time. A COCOM is a command, with a broad continuing mission, composed of significant components of two or more services under a single commander. The two categories of COCOMs include geographic COCOMs and functional COCOMs. Geographic COCOMs are established when a large geographic area requires a single commander responsible for effective coordination of operations. Likewise, functional COCOMs are created for broad continuing functional missions requiring single responsibility for effective coordination of related global operations.[26]

A COCOM is charged with giving authoritative direction to subordinate commands and the forces necessary to carry out assigned missions, including authoritative direction over all aspects of military operations, joint training, and logistics; organizing and employing commands and forces within that command; performing necessary campaign planning; and coordinating and approving control of resources and equipment, internal organization, and training.[27] Simply stated, COCOMs are charged with ensuring unified action of all subordinate commands and forces in order to carry out assigned missions. Although a COCOM's definition has not changed over time, the concept of unified action has evolved. Unified action now extends beyond the Services and includes the synchronization of activities with other governmental agencies and international governments, as well as with NGOs and the private sector.

The COCOM structure is designed to be flexible and change as required, accommodating evolving U.S. national security requirements. To ensure this flexibility, Title 10 USC tasks the CJCS to review the UCP not less often than every two years and submit recommended changes to the President, through the Secretary of Defense. Since President Truman's approval of the first UCP on 14 December 1946, this flexibility has been used on no less than 36 occasions to adjust DOD's structure to compensate for changes in the national security environment.[28] Appendix A, *Dates Unified and Specified Commands Established Under the Unified Command Plan*, provides a complete list of changes made to the UCP since its inception.

Following the experience of World War II, DOD recognized the importance of unity of effort achieved through the unified command of U.S. forces and over the next 50 years, the UCP adapted to the changing strategic environment.[29] A review of the history of three functional combatant commands (USTRANSCOM, USSOCOM, and USAFRICOM) provides valuable insight into how the changing national security environment can lead to successful changes in the overall organization of the COCOM structure. World War II, the Berlin blockade, the Korean War, and the war in Southeast Asia all demonstrated the need for the United States to maintain a capable and ready transportation system for national security. In 1978, exercise Nifty Nugget exposed great gaps in understanding between military and civilian participants and, as a result, mobilization and deployment plans failed. Two major findings came out of Nifty Nugget. First, Transportation Operating Agencies (TOAs) need a direct reporting chain to the JCS. Second, the JCS needs a single manager for deployment and execution. As a result, the JCS formed the Joint Deployment Agency (JDA).

Although the JDA had responsibility for integrating deployment procedures, it did not have authority to direct the TOAs or Unified and Specified Commanders to take corrective actions. According to several independent studies on transportation, the DOD needed to consolidate transportation.[30] Consequently, on April 18, 1987, President Reagan ordered that DOD establish a Unified Transportation Command (UTC), the forerunner to US-TRANSCOM. This order, coming eight years after the JCS formed the JDA, demonstrated how the UCP could be used to assist DOD in compensating for a changing strategic environment. The idea for a unified special operations command had its origins in the aftermath of Operation Eagle Claw, the disastrous attempted rescue of hostages at the American embassy in Iran in 1980. The ensuing investigation, The Holloway Commission, cited lack of command and control and interservice coordination as significant factors in the failure of the mission. With concern mounting on Capitol Hill, the DOD created the Joint Special Operations Agency (JSOA) in 1984. This agency, however, had neither operational nor command authority over any special operations forces (SOF). The JSOA was unable to improve SOF readiness, capabilities, or policies—not what Congress had in mind as a systemic fix for SOF's problems.

At the same time, a few Capitol Hill visionaries were determined to overhaul SOF. They included Senators Sam Nunn (D-GA) and William Cohen (R-ME), both members of the Senate Armed Services Committee (SASC). Nunn and Cohen felt strongly that DOD was not preparing adequately for future threats. Nunn expressed a growing frustration with the services practice of reallocating monies appropriated for SOF modernization to non-SOF programs. Cohen agreed that the United States needed a clearer organizational focus and chain of command for special operations to deal with low-intensity conflicts. In October 1985, the SASC published the results of its two-year review of the U.S. military structure.[31]

By spring 1986, SOF advocates had introduced reform bills in both houses of Congress. On 15 May, Cohen introduced the Senate bill, co-sponsored by Nunn and others, which called for a joint military organization for SOF. The final bill, attached as a rider to the 1987 Defense Authorization Act, amended the Goldwater-Nichols Act and was signed into law in October 1986. For the first time, Congress mandated that the President create a unified combatant command. Congress clearly intended to force the DOD and the administration to face up to the realities of past failures and emerging threats.[32] Despite how it was stood up, since its activation, USSOCOM has consistently proven its ability to successfully conduct a wide range of special operations, from foreign internal defense missions during times of peace to counterterrorism direct action missions during times of conflict.[33] A more recent example of reorganization comes from the U.S. approach to Africa. On February 6, 2007, President Bush and Defense Secretary Robert Gates announced the creation of U.S. Africa Command (USAFRICOM). The decision was the culmination of a 10-year thought process within the DOD acknowledging the emerging strategic importance of Africa and recognizing that peace and stability on the continent impacts not only Africans, but the interests of the United States and international community as well. Yet, the department's regional command structure did not account for Africa in a comprehensive way, with three different U.S. military headquarters maintaining relationships with African countries. The creation of USAFRICOM enables DOD to better focus its resources to support and enhance existing U.S. initiatives that help African nations, the African Union, and the regional economic communities succeed. It also provides African nations and regional organizations an integrated DOD coordination point to help address security and related needs.

USAFRICOM's mission is to conduct sustained security engagement through military-to-military programs, military-sponsored activities, and other military operations as directed and in concert with other USG departments and agencies and international partners to promote a stable and secure African environment. DOD engaged directly with other USG departments and agencies to gain their support in assigning personnel to the COCOM's staff positions.[34] The structure of the USAFRICOM headquarters was designed to provide an appropriate mix of military and civilian personnel in order to facilitate a holistic USG interagency approach to stability in Africa. This interagency infused structure ensures that the expertise, experience, and unique perspective of interagency personnel would permeate throughout all directorates. Day-to-day interaction between DOD and interagency representatives was determined to be the best way to integrate the military and civilian elements. In this manner, USAFRICOM plans, programs, and standard operating procedures benefit from interagency peer review. At present, more than half of the 1,304 approved billets at USAFRICOM are filled by civilians. Although the vast majority of those civilian positions are DOD personnel, the staff also includes 17 representatives from 12 USG departments and agencies. The personnel and the skills they bring add value to USAFRICOM's programs as well as improve the synchronization and collaboration of other USG efforts in Africa.[35] This examination of USTRANSCOM and USSOCOM makes it is clear that changes in the national security environment can effectively be addressed with modifications to the COCOM structure. While USAFRICOM is a good model for whole-of-government cooperation in support of stability operations, the interagency simply does not have the capacity to fully support this model across the world in all geographic COCOMs. In fact, DOD officially requested that DOS fill 13 additional USAFRICOM positions; however, DOS officials will not likely be able to fill these positions due to personnel shortfalls.[36]

Fast forward from the inception of USTRANSCOM and USSOCOM to December 2005 and NSPD-44 where the President formally acknowledges that the stability of foreign states serves the broader national interests and recognizes stability operations as a necessary capability. DOD responded by issuing new policy and guidance in the form of DODD 3000.05, and later DODI 3000.05, but up until the publishing of the December 2008 UCP did little to address its organizational structure for planning and executing stability operations. As defined within the latest UCP,

DOD's solution for a structure was to assign all geographic combatant commanders the responsibility for planning and conducting military support to stability operations. While this change had the potential to improve the DOD's ability to plan and conduct stability operations, it has proven ineffective in addressing the fundamental challenge of interagency synchronization because other U.S. government agencies do not have the capacity to provide expertise to each military COCOMs. An alternative that must be given serious consideration is establishing a single functional COCOM assigned the mission of stability operations.

As already discussed, functional combatant commands are created for broad continuing functional missions requiring single responsibility for effective coordination of global operations. Stability operations are clearly broad in scope and global in nature, not confining themselves to the boundaries of any specific geographic COCOM. Validating this point, the February 2010 Quadrennial Defense Review (QDR) states that stability operations are not niche challenges or the responsibility of a single military department, but rather require a collection of capabilities as well as sufficient capacity from across the DOD and other agencies. The QDR also recognizes that stability operations are not fleeting, and as such the United States must expect that for the indefinite future, violent extremist groups will continue to incite instability and challenge U.S. interests.[37] The QDR makes it is clear that stability operations are broad, global, and an enduring mission, therefore justifying the establishment of a COCOM to oversee this vital mission.

By creating a U.S. Stability Operations Command (USSTABCOM) and assigning it traditional functional COCOM responsibilities, DOD would utilize the same model established for planning and conducting other broad, global, and continuing missions such as operations against terrorist networks and strategic deterrence. Furthermore, charged with developing an integrating a global campaign plan for stability operations, USSTABCOM could become the interagency focal point for a unity of effort for planning stability operations. Faced with capacity challenges, DOD's interagency partners can focus their limited capabilities on the staff of a single COCOM rather than attempting to staff all COCOM's Joint Interagency Coordination Groups (JIACG).

Modeled after USSOCOM, USSTABCOM would also accomplish certain Service-like functions to include organizing and training general-purpose forces. The command would also develop strategy, doctrine, tactics, techniques, and procedures for stability operations. Further following the USSOCOM model, USSTABCOM would interact with geographic COCOMs through a Regional Stability Operations Integration Cell (RSOIC). Utilizing the regional expertise and forward presence, the RSOIC would be a force multiplier in conducting global stability operation campaigns. The RSOIC would also be the conduit between geographic COCOMs and USSTABCOM enabling the flexibility needed for command relationships. USSTABCOM would address the challenges identified within USG's stability operations capability, providing interagency partners and NGOs with an organizational structure, a global campaign planning process, and the logistical infrastructure to synergize stability operations.

One possible course of action in establishing a functional combatant command to focus on stability operations would be to transform an existing command. Through an updated UCP, USJFCOM can be re-missioned and reorganized to focus on stability operations. USJFCOM's current mission of "providing mission-ready joint-capable forces and supporting the development and integration of joint, interagency, and multinational capabilities to meet the present and future operational needs of the joint force" is well suited for this new mission. Furthermore, USJFCOM already has a primary goal to make irregular warfare a core competency. To achieve this objective, JFCOM's leadership professed, "We must move swiftly to make irregular warfare a core competency of the U.S. military. We must develop a mastery of irregular warfare comparable to that which we possess in conventional and nuclear warfare, leveraging our conventional dominance to asymmetrically improve in irregular war." They further state, "We must urgently adapt our expeditionary and general purpose forces to fight the irregular and hybrid wars we will likely face for the foreseeable future."[38] Based upon their mission and goals, USJFCOM already has the basic organization (to include interagency liaisons) to execute the stability operations mission.

Re-missioned as U.S. Stability Operations Command, USJFCOM could be modeled after USSOCOM and given the dual responsibility to organize, train, and equip assigned forces to include budgetary authority. U.S. Stability Operations Command (USSTABCOM) will be DOD's lead functional combatant command providing interagency partners and NGOs with an organizational structure, a deliberate and crisis action planning process, and the logistical infrastructure to synergize stability operations. Further, following the USSOCOM model, USSTABCOM would interact with geographic combatant commands through a Theater Stability Operations Command (TSOC). Utilizing the regional expertise and forward presence the TSOC will be a force multiplier in conducting global stability operation campaigns. The TSOC will be the conduit between USSTABCOM and the geographic combatant command enabling the flexibility to achieve the proper command relationship.

Retasking USJFCOM with such a huge mission would undoubtedly impact its current mission set, which includes: (1) force provider, (2) joint trainer, (3) joint command and control/capability development, and (4) joint concept development and experimentation. These important missions would be reassigned to an expanded Joint Staff.

THE IMPERATIVE FOR CHANGE

It has been five years since S/CRS was established and four years since President Bush signed NSPD-44 charging DOS with coordinating and leading integrated USG efforts to prepare, plan for, and conduct stabilization activities. The reality is that numerous studies have established that DOS does not have the capacity to effectively execute its responsibilities, and DOD's current structure exacerbates the civilian capacity gap. Even if civilian capacity is increased, which would take Congressional and Executive branch support, those resources would still take time to put in place. A less optimistic outlook would indicate that building the necessary capacity within DOS is not just a matter of resources, but of many other factors including organizational culture, and may therefore not be possible at all. Unfortunately, these missions are so critical, and the United States does not have the luxury of time.

Independent of civilian capacity challenge, DOD will be the lead for conducting stability operations in non-permissive environments. As such, DOD must maintain a capability to prepare, plan for, and conduct stability operations. In fact, the 2010 QDR identifies increasing stability operations capacity in General Purpose Forces (GPFs) as a major initiative.[39] The framework used by DOD to improve its own capability should be used as the structure for the rest of the interagency to better use the civilian capacity that does exist. Using the flexibility provided by Title 10 USC, DOD can take a page from its own history and modify the UCP to address changes to the national security environment. Establishing USSTABCOM would provide a focal point for developing global campaign plans; training of general purpose force; and collecting and incorporating lessons learned into future stability operations missions. More importantly USSTABCOM would provide the focal point to leverage the limited interagency capacity, thus ensuring the United States is prepared to effectively execute the critical national security missions of the 21st century.

APPENDIX I
Dates Unified and Specified Commands Established
Under the Unified Command Plan

SAC   Strategic Air Command (SAC)   Dec 1946
A specified command. President Truman's approval of the first Unified Command Plan on 14 Dec 1946 recognized the already existing SAC and brought it under JCS control.

Disestablished 1 Jun 1992; most functions assumed by USSTRATCOM.

PACOM   Pacific Command (PACOM)   Jan 1947
Re-designated:
USPACOM   US Pacific Command (USPACOM)   Oct 1983

FECOM   Far East Command (FECOM)   Jan 1947
Disestablished Jul 1957; functions assumed by USPACOM
ALCOM   Alaskan Command (ALCOM)   Jan 1947
Disestablished Jun 1975.

EUCOM	European Command (EUCOM)	Mar 1947

Nominally a unified command, but almost wholly of Army composition.

USEUCOM	US European Command (EUCOM)	Aug 1952

NELM	US Naval Forces, Eastern Atlantic Mediterranean (NELM)	Nov 1947

A specified command. From Aug 1952 to Feb 1960, also the Navy component of USEUCOM. Thereafter, CINCNELM had the concurrent title of CINCUS-NAVEUR as the Navy component of USEUCOM. Disestablished Dec 1963.

CARIBCOM	Caribbean Command (CARIBCOM)	Nov 1947

Re-designated:

USSOUTHCOM	US Southern Command (USSOUTHCOM)	Jun 1963

Assumed USACOM's geographic responsibilities for the   Jun 1996
waters adjoining Central and South America.
Assumed USACOM's geographic responsibilities for the   Jun 1997
Caribbean Basin.

LANTCOM	Atlantic Command (LANTCOM)	Dec 1947

Re-designated:

USLANTCOM	US Atlantic Command (USLANTCOM)	Oct 1983

Re-designated:

USACOM	US Atlantic Command (USACOM)	Oct 1993

Expanded responsibilities, including all CONUS-based Army and Air Force combat units.
Re-designated:

USJFCOM	US Joint Forces Command (USJFCOM)	Sep 1999

Focus became transforming US military forces.   Oct 2002
Transferred geographic responsibilities to USEUCOM and USNORTHCOM.
Per the Secretary of Defense, USJFCOM will be disestablished by the end of August 2011.

USNEC	US Northeast Command (USNEC)	Oct 1950

Disestablished Sep 1956.

USAFE   US Air Forces, Europe (USAFE)   Jan 1951
A specified command. From Aug 1952 onward, also the Air Force component of USEUCOM.
Specified command status terminated Jul 1956.

CONAD   Continental Air Defense Command (CONAD)   Sep 1954
Originally designated a joint command; made a unified command in Sep 1958. With Canada, the North American Air Defense Command (NORAD) was established Sep 1957. CINCONAD also designated CINCNORAD. Disestablished Jun 1975; functions assumed by ADCOM.

USSTRICOM   US Strike Command (USSTRICOM)   Jan 1962
Assumed additional responsibilities, Dec 1963, under
added designation USCINCMEAFSA (Middle East,
Africa south of the Sahara, and South Asia).
Disestablished Dec 1971; original functions passed
to USREDCOM.

USREDCOM   US Readiness Command (USREDCOM)   Jan 1972
Disestablished on Sep 1987.

ADCOM   Aerospace Defense Command (ADCOM)   Jul 1975
A specified command. NORAD continued, with CINCAD
also designated CINCNORAD.
Disestablished Dec 86; functions assumed by USSPACECOM.

MAC   Military Airlift Command (MAC)   Feb 1977
Designated a specified command for airlift.
Terminated as a specified command Sep 1988.

USCENTCOM   US Central Command (USCENTCOM)   Jan 1983
Replaced the Rapid Deployment Joint Task Force, established Mar 1980.
USSPACECOM   US Space Command (USSPACECOM)   Sep 1985
Disestablished Oct 2002; functions assumed by USSTRATCOM

| USSOCOM | US Special Operations Command (USSOCOM) | Apr 1987 |

| USTRANSCOM | US Transportation Command (USTRANSCOM) | Jul 1987 |

FORSCOM   Forces Command (FORSCOM)   Jul 1987
Designated a specified command. Specified command status terminated Oct 1993;
then became the Army component of USACOM

USSTRATCOM   US Strategic Command (USSTRATCOM)   Jun 1992
Assumed missions of USSPACECOM   Oct 2002

USNORTHCOM   US Northern Command (USNORTHCOM)   Oct 2002
Assumed USJFCOM's homeland defense functions. Also assumed Bahamas, Dec 2008
Puerto Rico, US Virgin Islands, Turks and Caicos Islands from USSOUTHCOM

USAFRICOM   US African Command (USAFRICOM)   Oct 2008
Assumed responsibility for most of Africa from USEUCOM with the Horn of Africa and Sudan transferred from USCENTCOM and the islands of Madagascar, Comoros, Seychelles and Mauritius transferred from USPACOM. Egypt remains under USCENTCOM.

Notes

[1]Chairman of the Joint Chiefs of Staff, *Joint Publication 1: Doctrine for the Armed Forces of the United States*, (Washington DC: GPO, March 20, 2009), I-6.
[2]Ibid., I-7.
[3]Chairman of the Joint Chiefs of Staff, *Joint Publication 3-07: Stability Operations* (Washington DC: GPO, November 25, 2009), I-2.
[4]Ibid., I-2.
[5]Lawrence A. Yates, *The US Military's Experience in Stability Operations, 1798-2005, OP 15* of the Global War on Terrorism Occasional Papers (Fort Leavenworth, KS: Combat Studies Institute Press, 2006), 1.
[6]Ibid., 2.
[7]Ibid., 40.

[8]Robert M. Gates (speech, U.S. Global Leadership Campaign, Washington DC, July 15, 2008).

[9]Headquarters, Department of the Army, *Field Operations 3-07: Stability Operations* (Washington DC: Department of the Army, October 6, 2008), 1-11.

[10]Barack Obama, *National Security Strategy*, (Washington DC: The White House, May 2010). Information presented is a summary and analysis of the 2010 National Security Strategy.

[11]Robert M. Gates, *National Defense Strategy* (Washington DC: GPO, June 2008). Information presented is a summary and analysis of the 2008 National Defense Strategy.

[12]Chairman of the Joint Chiefs of Staff, *The National Military Strategy of the United States of America: A Strategy for Today; A Vision for Tomorrow* (Washington DC: GPO, March 2005). Information presented is a summary and analysis of the 2005 National Military Strategy.

[13]Barack Obama, *Management of Interagency Efforts Concerning Reconstruction and Stabilization* (Washington DC: The White House, December 7, 2005). Information presented is a summary and analysis of NSPD-44.

[14]Michele Flournoy, Department of Defense Instruction 3000.05, September 16, 2009. Information presented is a summary and analysis of DODI 3000.05.

[15]"Office of the Coordinator for Reconstruction and Stabilization," *U.S. Department of State*, http://www.state.gov/s/crs.

[16]George W. Bush, *Unified Command Plan*, (Washington DC: The White House, December 17, 2008), Table of Contents. The geographic COCOMs include: U.S. Africa Command (USAFRICOM), U.S. Central Command (USCENTCOM), U.S. European Command (USEUCOM), U.S. Northern Command (USNORTHCOM), U.S. Pacific Command (USPACOM), and U.S. Southern Command (USSOUTHCOM). The functional COCOMs include: U.S. Joint Forces Command (USJFCOM), U.S. Special Operations Command (USSOCOM), U.S. Strategic Command (USSTRATCOM), and U.S. Transportation Command (USTRANSCOM).

[17]*Joint Publication 1*, III-10 to III-12. USSOCOM performs the service-like functions including the following: (1) Organize, train, equip, and provide combat-ready special operations forces (SOF) to the other combatant commands and, when directed, conduct selected special operations, usually in coordination with the geographic combatant commands in whose area of responsibility the special operations will be conducted; (2) develop strategy, doctrine, and tactics, techniques, and procedures for SOF; and (3) prepare and submit recommendations and budget proposals for SOF.

[18]*Unified Command Plan*, 7, 9, 11, 13, 17, 20, 21, 24, 27, 32.

[19]U.S. Naval War College, *A Primer for: Guidance for Employment of the Force (GEF), Joint Strategic Capabilities Plan (JSCP), the Adaptive Planning and Execution (APEX) System, and Global Force Management (GFM)*, (Newport, RI: Naval War College Press, March 24, 2009), 6-7.

[20]*Unified Command Plan*, 14-15, 24-25, 27-30.

[21]Flournoy, DODI 3000.05, 14-15.

[22]"USJFCOM Fact Sheet," *Joint Interagency Coordination Group*, http://www.jfcom.mil/about/fact_jiacg.htm. JIACG actions include participating in crisis

planning and assessments; advising on civilian agency campaign planning; providing civilian agency perspectives during military operational planning activities; presenting unique civilian agency approaches, capabilities and limitations to military campaign planners; and arranging interfaces for a civilian agency crisis planning activities.

[23]*George W. Bush, Presidential Report to Congress on Improving Interagency Support for United States 21st Century National Security Missions and Interagency Operations in Support of Stability, Security, Transition, and Reconstruction Operations* (Washington DC: The White House, June 2007); U.S. Government Accountability Office, *Stabilization and Reconstruction: Actions Are Needed to Develop a Planning and Coordination Framework and Establish the Civilian Reserve Corps* (Washington DC: GAO, November 2007); Cindy Williams and Gordon Adams. "Strengthening Statecraft and Security: Reforming U.S. Planning and Resource Allocation," *MIT Security Studies Program Occasional Paper, June 2008* (Cambridge: MIT Security Studies Program, June 2008); U.S. Government Accountability Office, *Military Operations: Actions Needed to Improve DOD's Stability Operations Approach and Enhance Interagency Planning* (Washington DC: GAO, May 2007); August 2006 *Interim Progress Report on DODD 3000.05, Military Support for Stability, Security, Transition, and Reconstruction Operations*; the April 2007 *Report to Congress on the Implementation of DODD 3000.05, Military Support for Stability, Security, Transition, and Reconstruction Operations*; and the May 2009 *Report to Congress on the Integration of Interagency Capabilities into Department of Defense Planning for Stability Operations.*

[24]*Integration of Interagency Capabilities*, 15.

[25]*Armed Forces*, U.S. Code 10 (2007), § 161.

[26]*Joint Publication 1*, I-14.

[27]Ronald H. Cole et al., *The History of the Unified Command Plan, 1946-1993* (Washington DC: Joint History Office, 1995), information presented is an updated version of Appendix I, 127-129.

[28]Ibid., xv.

[29]Ibid., 1.

[30]Ibid., 101-104.

[31]C. Lincoln Hoewing, "Defense Organization: The Need for Change," *Public Administration Review*, 46, 1986, 185-188, http://www.jstor.org/stable/976172.

[32]United States Special Operations Command History and Research Office, *History: United States Special Operations Command History, 6th Edition,* (MacDill AFB, FL: March 2008), 5-7.

[33]U.S. Government Printing Office, *Assessing U.S. Special Operations Command's Missions and Roles,* hearing, June 29, 2006, before the U.S. House, Terrorism, Unconventional Threats and Capabilities Subcommittee, Committee on Armed Services (Washington DC: GPO, June 29, 2006), 33.

[34]"About U.S. Africa Command," *U.S. Africa Command,* http://www.africom .mil/AboutAFRICOM.asp.

[35]*Integration of Interagency Capabilities*, 10-11.

[36]U.S. Government Accountability Office. *Defense Management: Actions Needed to Address Stakeholder Concerns, Improve Interagency Collaboration, and Determine*

Full Costs Associated with the U.S. Africa Command, U.S. House, Subcommittee on National Security and Foreign Affairs, Committee on Oversight and Government Reform, (Washington DC: GAO, February 2009), 5.

[37]Robert Gates, *Quadrennial Defense Review Report* (Washington DC: Department of Defense, February 2010), 20.

[38]"Command Mission and Strategic Goals," *United States Joint Forces Command,* http://www.jfcom.mil/about/priorities.htm.

[39]Gates, *Review Report,* viii.

The Strategic Impact of the Security Assistance Program in Contingency Operations

by Harvey R. Robinson

ABSTRACT

The Security Assistance Program is vital to building partnership capacity and supporting the National Security Strategy. Likewise, the Foreign Military Sales (FMS) program is a major pillar within the Security Assistance Program. FMS is used to provide the necessary resources to help strengthen the defense capabilities of United States' allies. However, the current FMS system was designed to support a Cold War adversary, not contingency operations. Following 9/11, the national foreign policy of the United States shifted to combating global terrorism. This policy shift resulted in the United States' involvement in contingency operations in Afghanistan and later in Iraq. The involvement in contingency operations also changed the focus to accelerating the FMS program to support the combatant commander during wartime. Therefore, the FMS system must be flexible and responsive to meet the increased demands from two simultaneous wars. It is inevitable that the United States will continue to face counterinsurgency operations; therefore, there needs to be an institutionalized mechanism for expediting the FMS process to achieve the United States national security objectives.

INTRODUCTION

We cannot do it alone in this world. We need friends and partners with the right capabilities to take care of their own security, to contribute to regional security, and through that relationship have the ability when it is appropriate... to join us in operations against common threats and enemies.[1]

 —*Mr. Bruce Lemkin, Deputy Undersecretary of the U.S. Air Force, International Affairs*

The United States has been involved in counterinsurgency operations in Afghanistan and Iraq for almost nine and seven years respectively. As of June 2010, the war in Afghanistan superseded the Vietnam War as the longest war in the history of the United States. Al-Qaeda and other extremist groups employ terrorism as a tactic with an overarching objective of undermining democracy in both Afghanistan and Iraq. Preventing the rise of global terrorism requires the United States to use all elements of national power to build partnerships and promote stability. The Security Cooperation Program is one program to help build partnership with foreign allies in order to strengthen alliances. Most importantly, the Security Cooperation Program is instrumental in supporting the objectives of the President's National Security Strategy.

Beneath the umbrella of the Security Cooperation Program is the Security Assistance Program. This program provides "the means through which the United States provides defense articles, military training, and other defense-related services to eligible foreign governments or international organizations by grant, loan, credit, or cash sales to further the United States' national policies and objectives."[2] According to a senior civil servant from the Office of the Secretary of Defense (Policy), "the Security Assistance Program is the foundation for the Security Cooperation Program."[3] Furthermore, the Security Assistant Program has strategic implications because according to the Security Assistance Management Manual (SAMM), "it serves as a fundamental instrument for achieving United States foreign policy objectives, and any assistance furnished under the program must strengthen United States national security and promote world peace."[4] In whatever capacity this vital program is used to strengthen alliances, the United States' laws, as well as national and foreign policy objectives, will determine how and when the Security Assistance Program is implemented. Every president since Harry

Truman has used Security Assistance Programs to further U.S. national interests.[5]

Yet, the wars in Afghanistan and Iraq have exposed some capability gaps in the programs' ability to effectively support contingency operations. The challenges of increasing the size of the host nation security forces in these wars prompted a request from the Central Command (CENTCOM) commander to accelerate the security assistance program, in particular the Foreign Military Sales (FMS) process. FMS is one of the six major components of the Security Assistance Program and it "provides the necessary equipment and training needed to sustain or influence a country."[6] The request to accelerate getting equipment and training to Afghanistan and Iraq simultaneously, as well as supporting the United States security objectives with its other allies, has put a strain on the Security Assistance Program. The problem is the Security Assistance Program was designed to build long-term relationships to help protect against a Cold War adversary—not to support contingency operations where units are engaging in combat operations.

Above all, the United States is at war and the security cooperation community must ensure that the FMS process is responsive enough to meet the increased demands to support the host nation in contingency operations. Legacy metrics must be revised to create conditions to make the system more responsive and less bureaucratic. Furthermore, the lack of interagency communication, insufficient training, and a Cold War mentality also is a source of friction within the security cooperation community. While all of these factors may influence how the FMS system operates, this chapter will specifically address the importance of the Security Assistance Program, and propose streamlining the case development and contracting segments of the Army FMS process to effectively support contingency operations.

THE SECURITY ASSISTANCE PROGRAM

Understanding the history of the Security Assistance Program is important to understanding the challenges the security cooperation community faces today. The beginning of Security Assistance can be traced to the Lend-Lease Program of World War II, when President Franklin D. Roosevelt pushed for the creation of the Lend-Lease Act. When the Act became law in March of 1941, it allowed for "the lend-lease or disposal of supplies needed by any country whose security was vital to the defense of the United States."[7] This new law provided the official means by which allies of the United States, such as Great Britain, the Soviet Union, and other countries, were supplied during the duration of the war. After World War II, the United States sought a new national strategy that did not involve actual military combat. A change, however, in U.S./Soviet relations meant a tougher U.S. line against Soviet expansionism.[8]

The focus on containment of communism led to the Truman Doctrine which was adopted in response to communist threats to Greece and Turkey. In a 1947 address, President Truman recommended providing aid to Greece and Turkey. He stated, "I believe that it must be the policy of the United States to support free people who are resisting attempted subjugation by armed minorities or by outside pressures."[9] The Truman Doctrine committed the United States to offer assistance to another country if it was in the best interest of the United States. Also, in an effort to repel the advancement of communism, the Marshall Plan was used to rebuild Europe, specifically Germany. The Marshall Plan's economic aid ended in 1952, returning every participating country to pre-war economic status, if not improving their economic status.[10]

Furthermore, with the focus still on the containment of communism and foreign relations, President Truman used his 1949 inaugural primarily to address foreign policy, and to "initiate the development of several programs, which we now collectively call security assistance."[11] The Mutual Defense Assistance Act of 1949 (MDAA) also shaped what conditions aid could be dispersed to allies in the quest to deter and resist Soviet expansion.

President Truman's administration used the MDAA to create a Military Assistance Program (MAP), with a budget of $1.3 billion directed primarily to NATO countries. This was the first truly global postwar military aid that allowed the president to sell military equipment, training and technical assistance, military construction projects, and military equipment transferred on a reimbursable basis to formal allies of the United States. The MAP provided the initial legal foundation for major security assistance programs that continued, in some form, throughout the Cold War and beyond.[12]

The outbreak of the Korean War in June of 1950 led to President Truman's approval of the National Security Council 68 report (NSC-68) in September 1950. One of NSC-68's major objectives was to assist U.S. allies to improve their militaries.

The Korean War, with its new "boots on the ground" philosophy, began a new era of how the United States would react to communist aggression. Also during this time the use of security assistance gradually shifted from Europe to Asia. The Security Assistance Program provided the aid needed to improve the defense capabilities of the United States' allies. As a result, less U.S. troops needed to be committed to support allies.[13] As Dr. James Lindsay, a U.S. foreign policy expert at the Council on Foreign Relations said, "it is cheaper to deploy a foreign soldier than an American soldier."[14] Following the Korean War, the United States reassessed the containment policy and eventually included non-allied but friendly nations in the roles of those who received U.S. foreign aid.[15] Throughout the Cold War, the United States continued to focus on containing communism, with security assistance remaining an integral part of its foreign policy. Since the support to U.S. allies during the Cold War was a long-term commitment, the process used to get the necessary equipment and training could take months, or even years. This long-term Cold War mentality existed well into the post-Cold War era within the security cooperation community.

The collapse of the Soviet Union eroded the original core rationale for the Security Assistance Program, but the Clinton administration and the following Bush administration continued to justify security assistance with three central arguments. First, security assistance helps friendly countries defend themselves against external and internal threats. Second, the programs strengthen the economies of friendly nations and advance U.S. economic interests. Third, security assistance promotes regional stability and maintains the cohesion of U.S. alliances, as well as being a tool for democracy promotion.[16]

After the terrorist attack on September 11, 2001, the United States shifted its focus and resources to fighting a war against terrorism. On December 11, 2001, President Bush said, "the need for military transformation was clear before the conflict in Afghanistan, and before September the 11th. What is different today is our sense of urgency—the need to build this future force while fighting a present war. It's like overhauling an engine while you are going at 80 miles an hour. Yet we have no other choice."[17] This sense of urgency is still important for all agencies supporting contingency operations. The agencies must remain flexible and adapt to the increased requirements needed to prevail in the current wars in Afghanistan and Iraq. Unlike the Cold War, time is now a crucial factor in getting the necessary resources to support the combatant commander in a wartime environment. Yet the security assistance programs at disposal of policymakers remain those forged in the Cold War crucible where timeframes sometimes encompassed years. The United States strategy of increasing indigenous Afghan and Iraqi security forces requires an acceleration of the Security Assistance Program, specifically FMS.

THE IMPORTANCE OF THE SECURITY ASSISTANCE PROGRAM AND FOREIGN MILITARY SALES IN TODAY'S OPERATIONS

It is important to ensure that the United States and Allied forces have the right equipment and training needed to conduct contingency operations. With the hard power assets of the United States stretched between two wars, humanitarian relief efforts, and supporting contingency operations, a multi-dimensional approach is needed to be successful. This approach includes partnering with legitimate host nation government forces because a unified approach is needed to meet the strategic objectives for the United States.

The Security Assistance Program is a force enabler for the combatant commander because it speeds the transition of friendly and allied countries to greater national self-reliance. Building partnership with allies helps protect the U.S. national interest. The use of the security assistance program to build partnership capacity also supports two objectives of the 2008 National Defense Strategy, which are to "promote security and deter conflict."[18] FMS contractors help reduce military footprint for logistics and training, and is a procurement strategy that allows a country to obtain defense articles using the U.S. Defense Acquisition System. The FMS program provides equipment and services needed to train and supply the Afghan and Iraqi security forces to aid in protecting their own population against both internal and external threats. Aside from providing equipment and training, the United States is looking for Afghanistan and Iraq to assume the primary responsibility of providing the manpower for its defense. For example, on December 1, 2009, President Obama unveiled his Afghanistan and Pakistan strategy at his first address to the Nation at the West Point Military Academy in New York. He made it clear that the United States strategy is "to train competent Afghan Security Forces, and to partner with them so more Afghans can get into the fight. And they will help create the conditions for the United States to transfer responsibility to the Afghans."[19] The same can be said for the strategy in Iraq.

The shift toward increasing security forces in Afghanistan and Iraq and the simultaneous long-term sustainment of U.S. forces and allies has placed tremendous emphasis on accelerating the FMS process. Iraq became eligible to receive foreign military sales and assistance in 2004, and Afghanistan in 2002. Vice Admiral Jeffrey Wieringa, head of the Pentagon's Defense Security Cooperation Agency (DSCA), confirmed President Obama's commitment to building partnerships, saying, "We sell stuff to build relationships, noting that United States partners needed the right equipment and training to carry out their security missions."[20] The intent is to transition security to a legitimate host nation government so that international troops can redeploy faster to insure that the host nation government's legitimacy is not undermined. As the Afghan and Iraqi security forces get stronger, the rate of American withdrawal can become greater. The efficacy of security assistance programs, therefore, will prove the lynchpin in U.S. success or failure in both these operations, and those to come.

FMS is also crucial to U.S. national security interests. FMS sales started at very low levels in 1950 and gradually increased to a multi-billion dollar program. Figure 1 shows the increase of resources in Afghanistan. The FMS sales in the table includes FMS cases paid by the host country and money allocated by the U.S. Government (USG) to purchase equipment for these countries, but excludes military construction cases. Pakistan is included to show the United States commitment to partner with them to help fight the war against terror in the region.

Countries	Sales (5M)			
	FY 06	**FY 07**	**FY 08**	**FY 09**
Afghanistan	$1,360.2	$2,065.0	$3,447.9	$3,480.9
Iraq	$343.8	$1,173.3	$1,337.6	$1,303.3
Pakistan	$55.8	$98.5	$229.3	$190.2
Total	$1,759.8	$3,336.8	$5,014.8	$4,974.3

Figure 1: Army FMS for Afghanistan, Iraq, and Pakistan[21]

RESPONSIBILITIES AND AUTHORITIES FOR SECURITY ASSISTANCE

All branches of the United States Government (USG) have a role in the Security Assistance Programs; however, the Department of State (DOS) and the Department of Defense (DOD) are the two principal agencies. DOS is responsible for the oversight of support to foreign countries because "they are the lead agency in formulating and implementing the United States' foreign policy and diplomatic relations."[22] The DOD "establishes military requirements and implements programs to transfer defense articles and services to eligible foreign countries and international organizations."[23] The Security Assistance Program is vital in "furnishing countries with the equipment, services, and training to defend them from aggression and enable them to operate alongside United State forces in a multinational effort."[24] Since two different agencies are central to the process, interagency communication is paramount in establishing an efficient and responsive system.

The Security Assistance Program is governed by the Foreign Assistance Act of 1961 (FAA), as amended and the Arms Export Control Act of 1976 (AECA), as amended. In addition to legislation, DSCA develops and implements policy guidelines and Congress provides oversight. The FAA is an "Act to promote the foreign policy, security, and general welfare of the United States by assisting peoples of the world in their efforts toward economic development and internal and external security, and for other purposes."[25] The FAA gives the Secretary of State the authority to "determine whether there shall be a security assistance program and the value of the program."[26] The transfer of defense articles, services, and training to allies increases interoperability, but the USG limits access to the most sensitive equipment, software, and technology. This limited access is governed by the AECA which "authorizes the President to control the import and export of defense articles and services, to designate such items as constituting the U.S. munitions list, and promulgate implementing regulations."[27] Security assistance can be a double edged sword if not wielded carefully as a foreign policy tool.

FMS is a multi-billion dollar program and, according to a senior DSCA civil servant representative, "there have been no major changes to the FMS process during the post Cold War era."[28] Furthermore, the last major legislative change to security assistance was in 1976. While the system essentially remains unchanged, DSCA and other agencies has established and led several Lean Six Sigma initiatives and integrated process teams (IPTs) to improve the efficiency of the FMS process from case development to delivery, five of which are pertinent to this chapter. First, DSCA established a Case Writing Division (CWD) at Wright-Patterson Air Force Base in March 2007 based on a recommendation by the Business Efficiencies and Action Team (BEAT). The team estimated that it cost over $3M annually to write 4,500 Letters of Offer and Acceptance (LOAs), Amendments, and Modifications, but they could save $1.2M per year if the case writing functions were consolidated from twenty different locations into a single DOD group led by DSCA.[29] The intent was to save resources without compromising service. In an effort to continue to improve the efficiency of the CWD, a DSCA policy letter 09-03, dated October 8, 2009, highlighted the primary responsibilities of the CWD and the Implementing Agencies (IA) in the case development process.

Second, the United States Security Assistance Command (USASAC) established an Intensive Management Office (IMO) in February 2007.[30] USASAC is the "Army's focal point for the development and execution of FMS for material and services. USASAC supports 140 allied countries, friendly nations and multinational organizations."[31] The IMO is designed to manage and push critical FMS cases for Afghanistan, Iraq, and Pakistan through the existing FMS process. An IMO was also established at each one of the Life Cycle Management Commands (LCMC) within the Army Materiel Command to ensure this benefit rippled throughout the Army's process.

Third, DSCA created the Security Cooperation Management Suite (SCMS) to provide better visibility and more complete information to a wide variety of U.S. agencies and war fighters. The SCMS provides the community a vertical-Theater, DSCA, service, Commodity Command, Geographic Combatant Command, Office of Secretary of Defense, and Joint Staff interactive, web-based collaborative tool to ensure that the FMS process, service contracting and defense transportation systems are effectively bundled into a flexible and responsive solution for requirements generated by real-time Stability, Reconstruction, and Contingency Operations.[32]

Fourth, the Pakistan, Afghanistan, Iraq, and Lebanon (PAIL) Task Force was created and according to COL Dave Dornblaser, USASAC, IMO Director for Afghanistan and Pakistan, this is an initiative chaired by the Office of the Secretary of Defense, Policy (OSD-Policy). The PAIL Task Force was organized to embrace all the current issues in these countries. This initiative involves members from various agencies and provides a forum to discuss any issues or concerns which can help improve interagency communication and improve the efficiency of FMS.

Fifth, Army Contracting Command (ACC), formally the Army Contracting Agency (ACA), was reorganized in October 2008. The once decentralized contracting centers within the Army Materiel Command (AMC) Life Cycle Management Commands (LCMCs) are now under one command. The ACC Commander "has directive authority over all Army contracting capabilities and provides a single focal point for status and readiness of the Army-wide contracting workforce."[33] A common theme running through many of these improvements, including the ACC, is consolidating individual nodes within the process. These improvements, while welcome, do not go far enough in a process of enormous complexity. In order to appreciate both the problem and what needs to be done, one must have a basic understanding of the FMS process.

KEY SEGMENTS OF THE FMS PROCESS

The security cooperation community is working on options to accelerate the FMS process and make it more efficient and responsive to the Combatant Commander during wartime. However, due to the complexity of the system, the FMS process is still not as efficient and responsive as it can be. Even though knowledge and training is not a direct function of the FMS process, there is evidence from surveys and interviews that indicate the lack of knowledge and training could impede the case development process. Each segment will be briefly discussed, but the focus is on the case development and contracting segments because modifications in these two areas will help accelerate the FMS process. The Letter of Offer and Acceptance (LOA) case development is the first step in the FMS process. This is a complex process because each FMS case must pass through several agencies before the case can be written and offered to the country. However, it begins when an eligible foreign country makes a request usually in the form of a Letter of Request (LOR) or for Afghanistan it is a Memorandum of Request (MOR) to the USG on items or services being considered for purchase. The LOR or MOR is used to develop the LOA.

The LOA is a contractual sales agreement between the United States Government and the foreign government or international organization, and it is the foundation of any United States government-sponsored sale of defense articles or services. The LOA is written by a U.S. Military Department (MILDEP) or other United States government implementing agency (IA), based on applicable regulations and the specifications the purchaser has set forth in its LOR.[34]

Before March 1, 2001, the case development process from LOR to LOA was 60 days. In a step backwards, however, this metric was changed from 60 days to 120 days.[35] According to the DSCA policy letter dated February 15, 2001, "this new measure analyzes a much broader scope including implementing agency, customer, DSCA and Security Assistance Officer (SAO) processing times."[36] The attempt to accelerate the FMS process to get equipment to the Afghan and Iraqi security forces faster drew attention to the 120 day metric, since the LOA is the first step in getting the necessary equipment and training needed to build these security forces.

During the case development process, both the Afghan and Iraqi Ministries should be involved because according to the Security Assistance Management Manual (SAMM), the purchaser should be involved early in the LOA development process to ensure requirements are clear and understood prior to offering the case for acceptance. The [implementing agency] should provide sufficient details in the LOA to allow U.S. contracting officers to nego-

tiate and award contracts without requiring foreign country representation or direct involvement in the formal negotiation
process.[37]

Another related key to success is a well defined requirement. A poorly defined requirement results in the country not getting the right equipment, or a delay in getting the equipment,
because time is wasted going back-and-forth between the purchaser and the Life Cycle Management Commands identifying the
proper technical specifications for the requested item. At the end
of the day, FMS is about providing the right capabilities at the right
time to the host nation to improve its capacity.

Constitutional separation of powers ultimately means that
Congress is responsible for legislative and oversight of the Security
Assistance Program. This oversight can come in the form of reports
or actual notification before a sale can occur if certain thresholds
are triggered. For example, "Congressional notification is required
for Major Defense Equipment (MDE) $14 Million or greater, non-
MDE $50 Million or greater, and for construction $200 Million or
greater."[38] Congressional notification is governed by the Arms Export Control Act of 1976, and any case requiring notification must
be reviewed by the Defense Security Cooperation Agency and the
State Department before going to Congress. Subsequently, Congress
has fifty days to approve or disapprove the FMS case, and the LOA
cannot be offered to the country without Congressional approval.

Interagency checks and balances occur at all levels of the
FMS process starting with the implementing agency. Each FMS
case passes through several agencies during the LOA development
process. Consequently this requires interagency unity of effort and
prioritization due to the number of competing requirements. However, achieving unity of effort requires an institutionalized approach so everyone is working within the same strategic
framework.

To accelerate the FMS process, the security cooperation
community reduced the amount of time each agency has to review
the FMS case and implemented temporary procedures that are resource and management intensive. For example, USASAC has two
days for Iraq and one day for Afghanistan instead of fifteen days
to complete the LOR technical review. However, whether a requesting country will need a waiver, additional documentation such as

a country team assessment or Congressional notification, depends on the type of equipment being requested, the value of equipment, and if United States taxpayers' money is used to fund the requested equipment or training. These checks and balances are designed to protect U.S. national interests. However, when time is precious to win over the host nation population and build partner capacity, these checks and balances should occur at a pace that does not impede the case development process.

The security cooperation community is focused on the case development process, but contracting and production is another important part of the FMS process. Ultimately, the contracting process plays a huge role in expediting the FMS cases because it is the longest part in the process. There is no separate procurement process for FMS and, according to a USASAC representative, "the Army does not have a warehouse full of major end-items; therefore, most of the defense articles purchased through FMS must be procured."[39] During wartime, the focus needs to shift to identifying urgent operational needs, finding ways to fill them, and moving the process along as quickly as possible. However, the use of FMS is significant because goods and services for foreign countries can be purchased through an already established acquisition program using Foreign Military Funds or USG Funds. In contracting, everything cannot be urgent, but there needs to be a system where senior leaders in DOD or the State Department can determine which requests are urgent, which could then fast track those requests into a separate process.

The security cooperation community needs to look at the rapid acquisition process and see if there are measures or policies that can be incorporated to accelerate the FMS process. For instance, procurement experts told the House Armed Services Committee Defense Acquisition Reform panel on October 8, 2009, that the following three DOD strategies could apply to many situations in which the department needs to buy systems quickly: 1. At the start of a rapid acquisition, officials must assess the immediate need, determine minimum requirements, and agree on a plan and stick to it, and not interrupt the acquisition and production processes to make changes, according to Thomas Dee, director of the Joint Rapid Acquisition Cell at the Office of the Undersecretary of Defense for Acquisition, Technology and Logistics. 2. Stay with the familiar proven technologies instead of testing new ones and according to Brigadier General Michael Brogan, commander of the Marine Corps Systems Command, this kept them from having to deal with requirements creep. 3. Relieve vendors of some of the work, if possible such as government adding the final pieces of equipment, such as radios. This will help get the equipment to the battlefield more quickly, according to Michael Sullivan, director of acquisition and sourcing management at the Government Accountability Office.[40]

In addition to these suggestions, establishing more indefinite delivery/indefinite quantity (IDIQ) contracts based on common types of equipment used in Afghanistan and Iraq will help accelerate the contracting process. An IDIQ contract allows the government to negotiate in advance for an indefinite quantity of services during a fixed period of time. Another advantage of IDIQ contracts is that the process of defining the requirement is eliminated, and the long bidding process has already been completed. IDIQs do require planning to establish, a process that can take four to six months, but once established, they can greatly speed up the process. A similar tool, contracting can use is blanket purchase agreements (BPA) that can fill requirements for recurring needs for supplies and services.

At the strategic level, the defense industry is an integral part of contracting because there is no warehouse full of major defense equipment waiting to be issued; therefore, everything must go through the procurement process. According to COL Dornblaser, USASAC, IMO Director, production is another area that slows down the FMS process because one has to "consider competition with United States forces versus competition with commercial customers."[41] In addition to FMS being good for the U.S. defense industry, however, FMS can also bolster the U.S. economy by keeping production lines open longer that will help ensure job stability.

Another piece of the FMS puzzle with strategic implications is transportation—moving the FMS equipment from the point of origin to the final destination. FMS for Afghanistan and Iraq travels through the Defense Transportation System, managed by the United States Transportation Command (US-TRANSCOM).[42] During an average week, "USTRANSCOM conducts more than 1,900 air missions, with 25 ships underway and 10,000 ground shipments operating in 75 percent of the world's countries."[43] However, FMS accounts for only around ten percent of USTRANSCOM's missions and shipments.[44] With technological advances, the combatant commander is capable of getting near real-time in-transit visibility of equipment enroute to his area of responsibility which can be factored into his operational plan. However, according to a USTRANSCOM liaison officer, "it is imperative that the CENTCOM staff provide USTRANSCOM with a training and fielding plan to ensure the equipment arrives in-time to conduct security training missions."[45] Undoubtedly, this recommendation could apply to other combatant commands.

The need for training touches more than just the transportation portion of FMS. There is a small community that understands FMS and how it functions at all levels. Lack of training has been identified throughout the security cooperation community as an area that needs improvement. Cross training and communication among the various agencies needs to be encouraged throughout the FMS program. U.S. civilian and military personnel who rotate into Afghanistan and Iraq must be trained on the FMS process. According to a senior civil servant at OSD Policy, "Security assistance is not a career promoting field...maybe people need to have a career path."[46] When operating in a foreign country, overcoming language barriers and proper training are vital to the success. The same holds true for Security Assistance that has its own language and processes that require proper training and expertise. The Defense Institute of Security Assistance Management (DISAM) at Wright-Patterson Air Force Base, OH, has been sending mobile training teams to Afghanistan and Iraq to bridge the FMS knowledge gap. Since it is imperative that the Security Assistance advisors understand the FMS process, the DISAM model may be worth expanding.

IMPROVING THE FMS PROCESS

There are a number of agencies and organizations within the State Department, Department of Defense, and Congress involved in the FMS process. There are checks and balances at all levels of the FMS process to ensure a country is eligible to receive aid and to control the export of sensitive technology. While these checks and balances are important, the FMS process must still be responsive enough to support the combatant commander in wartime. Therefore, a survey consisting of thirteen questions was sent to the USASAC liaison officers in Afghanistan and Iraq, the Contracting Command, and officials at various levels of the State Department and DOD (see Appendix A for survey questions). Also personal and telephone interviews were conducted. All participants are/were involved in processing FMS cases for Iraq, Afghanistan, or both.

Although they do not receive media attention commensurate with their importance, Foreign Military Sales are a critical component to building host nation capacity in Operation Iraqi Freedom and Operation Enduring Freedom. The United States is approaching the transition phase in Afghanistan and Iraq. The intent is not to abandon Afghanistan or Iraq, but work to get these two countries to a suitable level especially militarily. Even though there have been drastic improvements in the Iraqi security forces, there is still a demand to accelerate the FMS process. Throughout the security cooperation community, however, FMS is still viewed as a long-term process. A culture change of being more responsive is needed when working FMS cases for 21st century operations.

According to the surveys, the accelerated FMS requests in Iraq are causing frustration throughout the security cooperation community because the expedited FMS LOAs are not being signed and implemented in a timely manner. The LOA must be signed and implemented before it can go to contracting because according to a DSCA official, "FMS cases are legally required to be self-funded," meaning that these sales cannot make or lose money.[47]

One concern consistently raised was that the 120 day metric for the case development process was too long for these counterinsurgency operations. Based on the surveys, 54 percent agreed that 120 days is an acceptable metric. However, according to the surveys, those who agreed with the 120 day metric also made comments similar to COL Chris Oliver, former Army Team Chief in Iraq, who claimed, "there should always be a method to get the equipment faster, but as the situation stabilizes, then 120 days is good enough."[48] In an effort to support the combatant commander, the security cooperation community has established a revised goal of completing 80 percent of LOAs and Amendments within 45 days for Afghanistan and 65 days for Iraq. This shows that the security cooperation community is trying to be responsive. On the other hand, expedited LOAs should not remain in country for months waiting on signature and implementation. According to a senior USASAC representative, "expedited LOA should not take more than 7-14 days to obtain the necessary signature and implementation."[49] Also, shifting from a linear process to a concurrent process is effective in expediting case development in the existing FMS structure. For example, cases requiring Congressional notifications are being prepared early in the case development process to prevent any delays on preparing the LOA.

Feedback from the surveys and interviews revealed that poorly defined requirements were a key factor in slowing the FMS case development process. This finding points to the lack of training and not having the right people involved in defining the requirements. However, this issue can be resolved. According to a senior civil servant at the United States Army TACOM Life Cycle Management Command (LCMC), involving a contracting officer early in the case development process, using in-country DOD Acquisition personnel, direct communication with the LCMC should mitigate this problem.[50] Just as much focus should be on contracting because streamlining the contracting segment will definitely accelerate the FMS process. The Afghan and Iraqi Ministries must also be involved early in the LOR process, even if doing so lengthens the time or negotiation involved in the front part of the process—host nation involvement and capacity building more than makes up for those tradeoffs.

There were mixed reviews on the surveys and interviews as to whether the Congressional notification process slows case development. However, Congressional notification should not slow case development if Congress is in session, and DSCA and the State Department continue working together to get the FMS case to Congress early in the case development process. Of particular note are IDIQ contracts, which in some cases are being allowed to expire. After they expire, it takes four to six months to renegotiate the contract. By the interagency partners working together, these USG departments can make the most of Congressional time when the Congress is in session.

The FMS process requires an institutionalized systemic

change that is less bureaucratic or a separate FMS process for urgent operational requirements. The current Case Development metric of 45 days for Afghanistan and 65 days for Iraq must not be a temporary fix—other complex operations surely await the United States in the days to come, and they will require a more agile approach to FMS. Contracting must be involved early in the case development process, especially when defining the requirement. The FMS process must be responsive to the Combatant Commander, especially during wartime, and establishing more IDIQ contracts and using more blanket purchase agreements are ways to increase the responsiveness. However, combatant commanders must be informed that equipment or services that are not already on contract or cannot be diverted from stock may take a little longer to get. Both the FMS process, and those who use it, must become more realistic.

During the initial planning phase of a contingency operation, the interagency organizations can establish a Contingency Action Planning Team that includes representatives from DOS, DOD, MILDEPs, contracting, legal, finance and input from the combatant commander's planning team to discuss the best ways to accelerate the FMS process before a conflict starts. This group could also discuss funding streams, existing contracts, estimate the type of equipment and training needed based on historical data from Afghanistan and Iraq, or other operations. The contingency list of equipment and training based on historical data can be vetted through the various agencies as well as the combatant commander's planning team, and then contracts can be established in anticipation of conflict.

Fighting two wars without a nation at war is difficult. According to Mr. Bert Liptak, TACOM LCMC, "some vendors are not willing to surge to meet FMS demands."[51] Without a full mobilization of the industrial base, the acquisition community must use the industrial bases that are available. Given that the United States is involved in two simultaneous conflicts, the IDIQ contracts could be set-up using non-standard equipment (which keeps them from competing against equipment requests from the U.S. military). Then, there should be IDIQ contracts established for parts supply for this non-standard equipment. The use of standard equipment is good for standardization and interoperability with the U.S. allies. This arrangement would be good for the U.S. and its partners:

> The use of nonstandard defense equipment or supplies of American firms, previously used by the Department of Defense but no longer in inventory may be encouraged, when these equipment and supplies are more suitable to the mutual security interests of the United States and the foreign governments.[52]

All of these changes require a concentrated effort. Continued emphasis from the senior civilian and military leadership on FMS is needed to institute change in the FMS process.

It is inevitable that the United States will continue to face counterinsurgency operations in the 21st century; therefore, there needs to be an institutionalized mechanism for expediting the FMS process. The system must be flexible in order to remain relevant to meet the increased demands from combatant commanders, yet still allow for Congressional oversight. The system must be less bureaucratic, and still have the necessary checks and balances to protect the United States national interests. Streamlining the FMS process will benefit the customer, but most importantly it will quickly enhance the capability of the combatant commander in a wartime environment.

Security assistance has been the cornerstone of the U.S. foreign policy since President Franklin D. Roosevelt pushed for the Lend-Lease Act, and if history is an indicator, it will continue to be an integral part of U.S. foreign and national security policy. Securing the homeland is a matter of national security, and assisting in building stronger allied defense capabilities will reduce the chance of conflicts which eventually could threaten U.S. interests. Therefore, the focus on accelerating the FMS program is vital to getting the right equipment and training to support complex operations in a timely manner. The Afghan and Iraqi security forces must be strong enough to defend their country once the United States withdraws, a goal that can only be achieved, at least in part, through FMS. Institutional changes within FMS, as well as changes within the case development and contracting process, must occur so that the lessons from the first decade of the 21st century are institutionalized. As the security assistance program changes through presidential administrations, the overall objective remains the same—to strengthen alliances in support of U.S. national security objectives.

APPENDIX A (Survey Questions)

1.a. Describe a successful/productive experience when you interacted with the FMS process?

1.b. What made the interaction successful/productive in your opinion?

1.c. Describe an unsuccessful/unproductive experience when you interacted with the FMS process?

1.d. What made the interaction unsuccessful/unproductive in your opinion?

2.a. In your opinion, is the 120 day processing time from Letter of Memorandum to Letter of Offer and Acceptance still acceptable to meet the needs for Afghanistan? Explain.

2.b. In your opinion, is the 120 day processing time from Letter of Request to Letter of Offer and Acceptance still acceptable to meet the needs for Iraq? Explain.

3. Does Congressional Notification slow down the case development process? Explain.

4.a. Do you think the Afghan Ministries should be involved in defining the requirements for the LOR? Explain your answer.

4.b. Do you think the Iraqi Ministries should be involved in defining the requirements for the LOR? Explain your answer.

5. In your opinion, what can be done to make defining requirements easier?

6. Other than a well define requirement, what can be done to improve the acquisition process to get the equipment to the customer faster?

7.a. In your opinion, does the Afghan Ministries approve of the FMS process? If yes, explain why and provide an example; if no, explain why not and provide an example?

7.b. In your opinion, does the Iraqi Ministries approve of the FMS process? If yes, explain why and provide an example; if no, explain why not and provide an example?

8.a. In your experience, on average, how long does it take to get a Letter of Offer and Acceptance (LOA) signed and implemented in Afghanistan?

8.b. In your experience, on average, how long does it take to get a Letter of Offer and Acceptance (LOA) signed and implemented in Iraq?

9. Tell me about an instance when a long production lead time for equipment affected operational objectives.

10.a. In your opinion, will Direct Commercial Sales work better than the FMS process in Afghanistan? Explain

10.b. In your opinion, will Direct Commercial Sales work better than the FMS process in Iraq? Explain

11. Tell me about an instance where the lack of knowledgeable FMS personnel caused a delay in the case development process?

12.a. Does FMS support to other countries impact the support to Afghanistan? Explain.

12.b. Does FMS support to other countries impact the support to Iraq? Explain.

13. Tell me three concerns or perceptions you have with the FMS process?

Notes

[1] Bruce Lemkin (Deputy Undersecretary of the United States Air Force, International Affairs), interview with Reuters, "U.S. Arms Sales Topping $40 Billion," June 17, 2009, ww.reuters.com/article/idUSN1744179620090617.

[2] Headquarters, Department of the Army, *Field Operations 3-07: Stability Operations* (Washington DC: Department of the Army, October 6, 2008), 5-1.

[3] Jason Colosky (Partnership Strategy and Stability Operations, Office of the Secretary of Defense for Policy), interview with author, January 15, 2009, Pentagon, Arlington, VA.

[4] Security Assistance Management Manual (SAMM) DOD 5105.38-M, 22nd Edition, 151.

[5] Duncan L. Clarke et al., *Send Guns and Money: Security Assistance and U.S. Foreign Policy* (Westport, CT: Praeger Publishers, 1997), 1.

[6] David Dornblaser (Chief of Intensive Management Office, United States Army Security Assistance Office), interview with author, January 12, 2010, Fort Belvoir, VA.

[7] "Lend-Lease Act (1941)," *Our Documents*, http://www.ourdocuments.gov/doc.php?doc=71.

[8] SAMM, 2.

[9] Aimee Sexton, "Student Activity: Harry Truman and the Truman Doctrine,"

Harry S. Truman Library & Museum, http://www.trumanlibrary.org/teacher/doctrine.htm.

[10]Barry Eichengreen, *The European Economy Since 1945: Coordinated Capitalism and Beyond* (Princeton, NJ: Princeton University Press, 2007), 57.

[11]SAMM, 1.

[12]*Send Guns and Money*, 34.

[13]Ibid., 7.

[14]Dr. James M. Lindsay (Senior Vice President, Director of Studies, and Maurice R. Greenberg Chair), lecture, October 28, 2009, New York City, NY. Quotation used with Dr. Lindsay's permission.

[15]SAMM, 29.

[16]*Send Guns and Money*, 2.

[17]George W. Bush (speech, Citadel, Charleston, SC, December 1, 2001).

[18]Secretary of Defense, *National Defense Strategy* (Washington DC: Department of Defense, June 2008).

[19]Barack Obama (speech, Washington DC, December 1, 2009).

[20]Andrea Shalal-Esa, "U.S. arms sales seen topping $40 billion," Reuters, June 17, 2009, www.reuters.com/article/idUSN1744179620090617.

[21]Keith Schaffner (United States Security Assistance Command), telephone interview with author, February 21, 2010. Graph information received.

[22]Government Printing Office, "Department of State and International Assistance Program," www.gpoaccess.gov/usbudget/fy03/pdf/bud20.pdf, 231.

[23]Defense Security Cooperation Agency, "Chapter 2: Responsibilities and Relationships," http://www.dsca.mil/samm/Chapter%2002%20-%20Responsibilities%20and%20Relationships.pdf, 45.

[24]*Stability Operations*, 5-1.

[25]U.S. Government Printing Office, *Legislation on Foreign Relations Through 2002* (Washington DC: GPO, July 2003), http://www.usaid.gov/policy/ads/faa.pdf, 18.

[26]DSCA, "Chapter 2," 45.

[27]SAMM, 504.

[28]Joe Lontos (Iraq Country Program Director, DSCA), telephone interview with author, January 12, 2010, Crystal City, VA. It should be noted that Mr. Jason Colosky, Partnership Strategy and Stability Operations, Office of the Secretary of Defense (Policy), stated, "there have been some Title 10 changes" in a January 15, 2009, interview at the Pentagon, Arlington, VA.

[29]DSCA, "Policy Letter 06-16," February 28, 2006.

[30]Jerome Barrett (former Deputy of the Intensive Management Office), interview with author, Fort Belvoir, VA.

[31]U.S. Army, "U.S. Army Assistance Command," www.USASAC.army.mil.

[32]*Journal of International Security Assistance Management* (Wright-Paterson, AFB: November 2009), Vol 31 Iss. 3, 14.

[33]"Army contracting command created," *Army Logistician*, May-June 2008, http://findarticles.com/p/articles/mi_m0PAI/is_3_40/ai_n27907764/.

[34]SAMM, 177.

[35]DSCA, "Policy Letter 01-06: New Metric to Measure LOA Processing Time Line

Performance," February 15, 2001.

[36]Ibid.

[37]*Journal of International Security Assistance Management*, 207.

[38]"Foreign Military Sales Case Development," *SAMM*, http://www.dsca.mil/samm/Chapter%2005%20-%20FMS%20Case%20Development.pdf, 236-238.

[39]Representative (U.S. Army Security Assistance Command (USASAC)), interview with author, December 26, 2009.

[40]Matthew Weigelt, "4 lessons in Rapid Acquisition Learned from DOD's New ATVs," October 15, 2009, http://fcw.com/articles/2009/10/19/acq-rapid-acquisition.aspx.

[41]Representative (USASAC), interviewed by author, December 13, 2009.

[42]USTRANSCOM provides strategic air and sea lift capabilities and it consists of the following commands: The Surface Deployment and Distribution Command, The Air Mobility Command (AMC), and The Military Sealift Command (MSC).

[43]"Mission," *U.S. Transportation Command*, www.ustranscom.mil.

[44]Barry Johnson (USTRANSCOM TCJ3 LNO), interview with author, March 18, 2010.

[45]Ibid.

[46]Colosky, interview, January 15, 2009.

[47]Lontos, telephone interview, January 12, 2010.

[48]Chris Oliver (Former U.S. Army Team Chief in Iraq), survey, January 18, 2010.

[49]Dornblaser, interview, January 12, 2010.

[50]Bert Liptak (Director of Security Assistance Management, U.S. Army Tank-automotive and Armaments Command Life Cycle Management Command), telephone interview with author, January 12, 2009.

[51]Ibid.

[52]SAMM, 144.

Piracy:
A Local Threat with Global Impact

by Matthew G. St. Clair

ABSTRACT

This study analyzes the global impact of Somali pirates and how non-state actors can flourish under the conditions of a failed state. The global economy depends on maritime trade and transport. Approximately 80 percent of world trade is conducted over sea lanes and 75 percent of oil tankers pass through strategic chokepoints.

Somalia is strategically located to the main Sea Lanes of Communication connecting Europe and Asia. Approximately 22,000 vessels sail through the Suez Canal, Red Sea, Strait of Bab el-Mandab, Gulf of Aden, and Arabian Sea annually. In 2008 Somali pirates collected over $30 million in ransom for vessels hijacked in territorial and international waters, caused nation-states to commit valuable naval and surveillance capabilities to patrol the Gulf of Aden, and provided over $1.5 million received as ransom to Al-Shabab, an Islamic fundamentalist group in Somalia with ties to al-Qaeda.

The goal of this study is to address some of the more important issues associated with piracy originating from Somalia and the threat of their potential cooperation with terrorist groups. Unless the international community acts in concert to address piracy, these non-state actors will continue to undermine the security of the global commons at will.

INTRODUCTION

Piracy and incidents of maritime crime tend to be concentrated in areas of heavy commercial maritime activity, especially where there is significant political and economic instability, or in regions with little or no maritime law enforcement capacity. Today's pirates and criminals are usually well organized and well equipped with advanced communications, weapons, and high speed craft. The capabilities to board and commandeer large underway vessels—demonstrated in numerous piracy incidents—could also be employed to facilitate terrorist acts.

—The National Strategy for Maritime Security, September 2005

In 2008, Somali pirates collected over $30 million in ransom for vessels hijacked in territorial and international waters, caused nation states to commit valuable naval and surveillance capabilities to patrol the Gulf of Aden, and provided over $1.5 million received as ransom to Al-Shabab, an Islamic fundamentalist group in Somalia. Somalia's continued status as a failed state, the inability of the Transitional Federal Government (TFG) to deter or prevent piracy operations, and the presence of terrorist groups already in Somalia, create ideal conditions supporting a possible nexus between Somali pirates and other non-state actors, specifically terrorists.[1]

Studying piracy is important as it is a transnational threat conducted by non-state actors that adversely affects the world economy and challenges political and security stability of nation states throughout the world.[2] The global economy depends on maritime trade and transport. Approximately 80 percent of the world trade is conducted over sea lanes and 75 percent of oil tankers pass through strategic chokepoints. "The sea is still the most practical and economic (sometimes the only) means of transporting large volumes of cargo, particularly those in bulk such as oil and other raw materials," notes one expert.[3]

The modern pirate is little different than the pirates who sailed the high seas in the 18th century during the golden age of piracy. Pirates are criminals preying on commercial and civilian mariners with the intent of hijacking vessels and stealing cargo. They challenge the authority of nation states and established international laws protecting the freedom of navigation on the maritime domain. Unlike the pirates of the past, modern pirates demand significant ransoms for returning hijacked vessels and crews.

Defining piracy today is not an easy task, however, in part because there are two internationally recognized definitions for piracy. The first definition is provided by the International Maritime Organization (IMO), the sanctioned agent of the United Nations (UN) to address law of the sea issues:

(a) Any illegal acts of violence or detention, or any act of depredation, committed for private ends by the crew or the passengers of a private ship or a private aircraft, and directed:

(i) On the high seas, against another ship or aircraft, or against persons or property on board such ship or aircraft;

(ii) Against a ship, aircraft, persons or property in a place outside the jurisdiction of any State;

(b) Any act of voluntary participation in the operation of a ship or of an aircraft with knowledge of facts making it a pirate ship or aircraft;

(c) Any act inciting or of intentionally facilitating an act described in sub-paragraph (a) or (b).[4]

The major problem with this definition is that it does not address acts of piracy committed within a nation's territorial waters where most acts of piracy occur. The IMO definition leaves jurisdiction for acts of piracy within territorial waters to be adjudicated by the nation state, which has enormous consequences when applied to a failed state such as Somalia. The weak and corrupt Transitional Federal Government of Somalia does not have the capability, and arguably the will, to capture Somali pirates, let alone hold them accountable in a court of law. Accordingly, Somali pirates operate freely within the territorial waters of Somalia.

The second commonly referred to definition of piracy is from the International Maritime Bureau (IMB) of the International Chamber of Commerce (ICC), which defines piracy as "an act of boarding or attempting to board any ship with the apparent intent to commit theft or any other crime and with the apparent intent or capability to use force in the furtherance of the act."[5] This definition is broader in scope, and does not delineate between acts of piracy conducted in territorial waters and those acts of piracy conducted in international waters. Although the United States and the majority of the international community observe the inadequate IMO definition for piracy, the IMB definition provides more flexibility to the international community to address all acts of piracy.[6]

The threat posed by Somali pirates extends beyond Somalia's territorial waters and the Horn of Africa. The criminal activities of Somali pirates have direct impact on the global market. Somali pirates threaten the very security of a major economic artery connecting Eastern and Western markets, all while operating in waters patrolled by warships of many of the world's major powers, to include the United States. These well organized, highly sophisticated gangs are fueling an already global financial crisis. If the shipping industry avoids transiting the Suez Canal to by-pass pirate infested waters, how will the world market respond to a significant delay in the supply and demand life cycle? What would the impact be on Egypt without the $5 billion in annual income from fees collected from maritime traffic transiting the Suez Canal?[7] These questions are not theoretical as Somali pirates ignore the rule of law of nation states, and are an example of the consequences for the world's acceptance of a failed state.

Somalia has remained a failed state since 1991, providing a sanctuary for criminals and terrorists while serving as an enabler for piracy. The potential for monetary reward is the root cause of piracy. The TFG is ineffective and does not have the leadership and resources to affectively address piracy. Therefore, Somali pirates operate at will, threatening the security and freedom of movement through international waters.

Somali pirates challenge international law without fear of reprisal from the TFG. On 8 April 2009, Somali pirates attempted to hijack the Maersk Alabama, a U.S. flagged vessel with a crew of twenty U.S. citizens. This was the first act of piracy directed toward the United States in over 200 years. This incident set the stage for a dramatic in extremis hostage rescue by U.S. Special Forces of the ship's captain who gave himself up as a hostage to the pirates in order to free his crew. Although the United States captured one pirate involved in the Maersk Alabama incident, few Somali pirates have been captured or brought to trial in accordance with the 1988 United Nations Convention for the Suppression of Unlawful Acts Against the Safety of Maritime Navigation (SUA Convention).[8]

These conditions have "emboldened them to strike further from the shore and move northwards into the Gulf of Aden, which links the Red Sea and Suez Canal to the Arabian Sea."[9] The capability to operate beyond Somalia's territorial waters is significant as it provides the pirates opportunities to hijack maritime vessels (MV) of strategic importance, such as oil tankers, and demand substantially higher ransoms.

Attacking the shipping industry is a lucrative business for Somali pirates and is also an ideal, yet unexploited, soft target for terrorist organizations. Global security has tightened due to Overseas Contingency Operations (OCO) led by the United States, and it is exceedingly more difficult for terrorists to attack traditional targets, forcing them instead to look for easier prey.[10] The threat to the shipping industry's security from Somali pirates and terrorists is significant as "nonstate actors—especially those whose actions defy the norms and values of the international community—will play an increasingly significant role. Nonstate actors undermine law and order, and...create conditions conducive to instability and conflict. For commercial traffic through chokepoints and SLOCs [Sea Lanes of Communication], pirates and maritime terrorists are the primary concerns."[11] A rapidly innovative enemy will exploit the operating environment to his advantage, which is exactly what is happening in the sea.

Although pirates and terrorists have different goals, the potential benefits from forming a nexus also increase the potential security risk of piracy. On 25 September 2008, Somali pirates hijacked the MV Faina, a Ukrainian owned vessel, transporting 33 Russian made T-72 tanks, small arms, and an assortment of ammunition. Although unlikely that the pirates would be able to move the tanks off the ship, they could remove the other weapon systems and ammunition selling them to the highest biding terrorist organization. The pirates desire financial gain while terrorist require weapons, ammunition, and safe havens from which to operate. That said, this cooperation would be a risky undertaking for the Somali pirates, adding a layer of complexity to their operations, inserting the influence of outside leadership, and gaining considerably more attention from the international community—arguably something that is not good for the pirates' business model.

The next section examines Somalia as a failed state and

assesses the scope and influence of Somali pirates. Then, the chapter addresses how a nexus between Somali pirates and terrorist groups might occur and the global impact of such a merger. This study concludes with an analysis of the challenges piracy poses to U.S. foreign policy, and provides recommendations for consideration in the on-going fight to combat piracy in Somalia.

SOMALIA AS A FAILED STATE

The seeds for Somali pirates were sown in 1991 when Somalia's government collapsed. War lords and clan leaders fought fierce battles to assert their dominance, but no single group emerged the victor. Fisherman from Europe and other African nations took advantage of Somalia's inability to patrol the coastline and began fishing in Somalia's abundant territorial waters. Groups of Somali fisherman armed themselves to protect their way of life and began attacking the foreign fishermen.[12] The Somalis eventually began to expand their operations to attack merchant vessels sailing through Somalia's territorial waters. The golden age of Somali pirates had begun while Somalia plunged further into chaos.

In 2004, the Somali Transitional Federal Government (TFG) formed in Kenya and was recognized as Somalia's legitimate government by many nation states, including the United States. However by 2006, a group of Somali Islamic fundamentalists, known as the Somali Council of Islamic Courts (CIC), began to wield considerable influence and controlled a significant portion of Somalia. The CIC established a judicial system based on Sharia law and provided police forces, receiving support from numerous clan leaders. The CIC actually reduced piracy operations by declaring it un-Islamic and shut down pirate base camps, something that no other group has accomplished since.[13] Somalis accused of engaging in piracy were tried in courts established by the CIC.

With the assistance of U.S. airpower, the TFG was able to eliminate the threat posed to their fragile government by the CIC. This was short lived, however, and the authority of the TFG was challenged by yet another Islamic fundamentalist group. Since early 2007, the leadership of Al Shabab has succeeded in establishing their authority throughout Somalia, but unlike the CIC, Al Shabab supports piracy. By all counts of good governance, the TFG has failed miserably, and on 20 December 2008, the TFG president,

Abdullahi Yusuf Ahmed, officially resigned. This creates favorable conditions for the Islamic jihadists of Al Shabab to assert its growing dominance in Somalia while continuing its support of Somali pirates.

Corruption runs deep within the TFG. Many officials, to include the president, received payments and kickbacks from pirates and traffickers to "look the other way" supporting Somali instability.[14] The hands of Somalia's ineffective law enforcement forces reach deep into the pockets of Somali pirates. Real power within Somalia continues to be exercised by clan leadership, Islamic militants, pirates, and other criminal organizations. Within their territory, or "turf," these groups control the rule of law and illicit trade, determining how monies are distributed and how they should be used.[15] Without a government with the will and capacity to stop piracy, piracy will continue to flourish, further threatening the security of the global market and freedom of navigation.

SCOPE AND INFLUENCE OF SOMALI PIRATES

Somalia is strategically located to the main SLOC connecting Europe and Asia. Approximately 22,000 vessels sail through the Suez Canal, Red Sea, Strait of Bab el-Mandab, Gulf of Aden, and Arabian Sea annually (See Figure 1). One-fifth of the world's oil tankers, one-third of containerized cargo, and one-half of the world's bulk cargo use the Gulf of Aden Sea lane supporting global commerce.[16] Somalia's 1,800 mile coastline provides Somali pirates with an ideal safe haven from which to plan and conduct operations. Somalia is also within proximity to Yemen which is a known juncture for al-Qaeda and other terrorist organizations.[17] The uninhibited access Somali pirates have to this strategic commercial sea lane leaves the shipping industry with few options. Maritime vessels must either continue to use the Gulf of Aden sea lane or make a significant deviation and sail around the southern tip of Africa and the Cape of Good Hope into the South Atlantic Ocean (See Figure 2). Such a deviation would come with a tremendous financial impact on the global market, shipping industry, and world consumers.[18] Utilizing a sea lane around the Cape of Good Hope would increase the time required to move seaborne commerce from Asia to Europe and the United States by five days, and an additional ten days from the Middle East. The shipping industry would experience an aver-

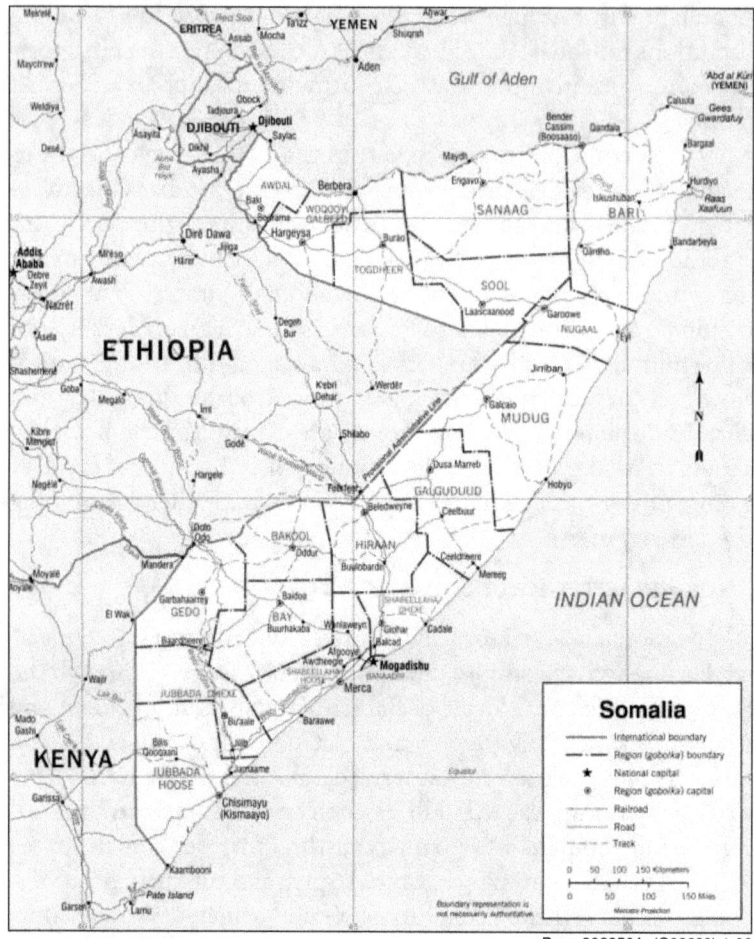

Base 802850A (C00298) 1-02

Figure 1: Map of Somalia
Source: https://www.cia.gov/library/publications/the-world-factbook /maps
/maptemplate_so.html

age increase of $30,000 in the daily operating cost of each commer-
cial vessel.[19] Lloyd's of London, a major underwriter of marine insurance policies, "declared the Gulf of Aden a war-risk zone subject
to a premium of tens of thousands of dollars per day."[20] Acts of
piracy originating from Somalia's shores threaten more than the
mariners operating the ships—these acts challenge the very security of the global market.

In general, there are three levels of piracy. Lower-level at-

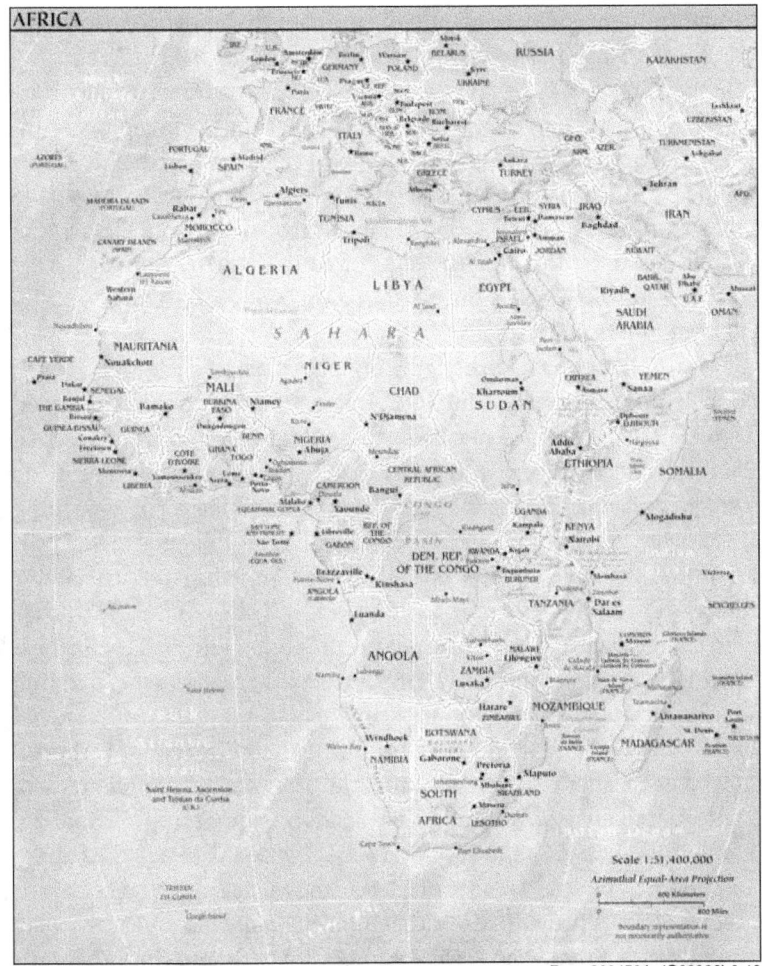

Figure 2: Map of Africa
Source: https://www.cia.gov/library/publications/the-world-factbook/reference_maps/africa.html

tacks are directed at vessels anchored in a harbor where port security in many countries is relaxed. The objective of lower level attacks is to steal cash and high value items. Mid-level attacks occur on vessels sailing in territorial waters or on the high seas where pirates seize the cargo of the ship. The highest level of attacks involves the hijacking of a vessel and its crew for the purpose of obtaining ransom money or selling the hijacked ship.[21] Somali pirates execute the latter two types of attacks, and more often than not are successful.

During the first nine months of 2008, the IMB reported 199 worldwide acts of piracy, with one-third of those attacks executed by Somali pirates. Currently Somalia is the leading piracy danger zone. Somali pirates conducted 63 attacks, 51 within the Gulf of Aden and 12 within Somali territorial waters.[22] During the period of November 10–16, 2008, Somali pirates conducted 11 attacks with three successful hijackings. As of June 17, 2010, Somali pirates were holding 17 vessels for ransom along with approximately 350 crew members as hostages.[23]

Somali pirates are highly organized and well equipped with Global Positioning System (GPS), speedboats, rocket propelled grenades, AK-47s, and machineguns. Attacks are either launched from the shore or from a "mother ship." The mother ship serves as a staging platform at sea from which to launch attacks by swarming the target vessel in small skiffs or speedboats. The mother ship allows pirates to attack vessels well beyond Somalia's territorial waters and into the strategic shipping lanes of the Gulf of Aden that feed the global market. Attacks are completed within 15 minutes, making it virtually impossible for international Navies patrolling the Gulf of Aden to respond in a timely manner.

Somali pirates do not coordinate their efforts nor is there a centralized leader or chain of command. They act independently and are legitimized by clan and tribal leaders supporting Al Shabab. These leaders, not the TFG, have the ability to influence the behavior of Somali pirates as most pirates acknowledge clan and tribal authority. Pirates provide income to build schools, mosques, and play grounds in their villages as well as inject life back into the local economy, something the TFG has failed to accomplish. The contributions of Somali pirates to the local economy replicate those of the Islamic Palestinian fundamentalist group Hamas in the Gaza Strip of Israel, and both groups enjoy widespread popular support within their respected communities. As long as pirates infuse money into their communities, those with authority to stop them will likely encourage more aggressive operations. However, it is unclear whether the clan and tribal leaders would approve of pirates cooperating with terrorist groups as this would bring increased international attention on the fishing communities for aiding terrorists.

Somali pirates are far from amateurs—they are extremely

skilled and knowledgeable mariners. Their maritime expertise and unhindered access to one of the world's busiest shipping lanes offer terrorists an option that may warrant further evaluation on how to exploit. Today there is significant evidence showing considerable links between terrorist groups and criminal organizations making their ideals and motivations increasingly difficult to differentiate.[24] In the case of Somali pirates being courted by terrorists, the possibility exists since there are potential benefits for each group.

The November 18, 2008, hijacking of the MV Sirius Star, a Saudi Arabian oil tanker carrying over two million barrels of oil worth in excess of $100 million, was hijacked over 400 miles from the Somali coast. This hijacking caused the Organization of the Petroleum Exporting Countries (OPEC) to immediately raise the price of a barrel of crude oil over one dollar to $58, demonstrating the global influence of Somali pirates.[25] The second and third order affects of piracy to the shipping industry are increases in insurance premiums and shipping rates, costing the industry anywhere from $500 million to in excess of one billion dollars annually.[26]

How would OPEC react if the MV Sirius Star was destroyed by explosives emplaced by a non-state actor such as al-Qaeda or other terrorist organization? Would Somali pirates, after receiving ransom payment from the company owning the vessel, allow members of a terrorist organization to board the MV Sirius Star and prepare it to be a seaborne improvised explosive device? Although unlikely, it is certainly within the realm of possibility that Somali pirates, for a price, would cooperate with non-state actors. This very real threat has "informed the perceptions of governments, international organizations, and major shipping interests around the world."[27] Given that al-Qaeda will target anything that would weaken its enemies, the global economy, in its eyes, is fair game.

No sanctions or international economic tariffs can stop this business. Globalization has placed greater demand on the shipping industry to ensure the strategic flow of resources supporting the global economy. According to the United Nations Conference on Trade and Development (UNCTAD), over the past three decades, world seaborne trade experienced an average growth rate of approximately 3.1 percent.[28] In 2007 alone, world seaborne trade increased by 4.8 percent from 2006 with an estimated 8.02 billion tons of goods shipped.[29] An increased volume of maritime trade provides Somali pirates with more lucrative targets and, thus, more potential income and incentive to expand their operations. Although attacks from Somali pirates have increased, their overall impact on annual maritime commerce that exceeds $7 trillion is rather insignificant.[30] A more significant economic impact may occur if the shipping industry determines it necessary to avoid the Somali pirate threat and instead navigates around the Cape of Good Hope. Several companies such as the Norwegian shipping company Odfjell SE and the American shipping company Maersk, one of the world's largest shipping companies, have already begun using this alternate route.[31]

The long arm of Somali pirates touches the world, and the pirates can largely act with impunity. Somali pirates are the symptom of continuous anarchy within a failed state and the lure of a lucrative illicit economy. They serve as a constant reminder of the power and influence yielded by a non-state actor on the international stage.

Piracy fuels the illicit economy of Somalia. It provides employment to the young, restless, military aged males who have no other opportunities that provide similar economic rewards as piracy. There are literally hundreds of pirates from the various coastal fishing villages, and this number will likely continue to increase as long as the opportunity of financial gain exists. Pirates are seen as heroes in most villages and are supported by clan leadership. The success enjoyed by Somali pirates over the past several years has caused villages and towns once living in poverty to now thrive with shops, restaurants, and even luxury cars, all through the monies obtained from piracy.[32] As long as the pirates are able to flourish under these conditions, there is no incentive for them to cease operations or cooperate with the TFG.

INFLUENCE OF TERRORIST GROUPS IN SOMALIA

Somalia offers the ideal sanctuary for non-state actors, specifically terrorist groups. It provides terrorists requiring "areas that combine rugged terrain, weak governance, room to hide or receive supplies, and low population density with a town or city near enough to allow necessary interaction with the outside world."[33] Osama Bin Laden created the Islamic Army Shura to enable him to coordinate with various terrorist groups with whom he was seeking alliances, and Somalia was one of twelve countries belonging to this organization.[34]

Al-Qaeda established a strong presence in Somalia and, in 1992, Bin Laden issued a fatwa demanding removal of all U.S. forces in Somalia supporting humanitarian relief efforts. As conditions in Somalia deteriorated, al-Qaeda provided training and resources to the warlords and Islamic militants that led to the deaths of 18 U.S. soldiers and the downing of two Blackhawk helicopters.[35] President Clinton began the withdrawal of U.S forces out of Somalia and reduced diplomatic engagement in Somalia, contributing to the U.S. foreign policy void that exists today.

In 1998, Bin Laden stated "that he and his followers had been preparing in Somalia for another long struggle."[36] According to the U.S. Assistant Secretary of State for African Affairs, senior leadership within Al Shabab has close ties with al-Qaeda and encourages terrorists to come to Somalia.[37] Al Shabab controls most of Southern Somalia and sections of Mogadishu. Should Al Shabab assume control of Somalia given the inability of the TFG to establish rule of law and effective governance, al-Qaeda and its affiliates may try to broaden the existing relationship with Al Shabab in order to use Somalia as a safe haven from which to launch future terrorist attacks.

The threat to the security of the Gulf of Aden shipping lanes becomes magnified if Somali pirates extend their services to these terrorist groups in order to increase pirate cash flow. Cooperation between Somali pirates and the Al Shabab/al-Qaeda partnership may be in the best interest of the pirates in order to continue operations under the rule of Islamic fundamentalists. A potential drawback for pirates cooperating with Al Shabab and al-Qaeda is that the pirates would receive considerably more attention from the United States and its allies in the prosecution of OCO which would significantly disrupt pirate operations. The short term monetary gains to be achieved by Somali pirates from cooperating with terrorists may, or may not, be worth the risk of being categorized as terrorists by the international community.

The U.S. led OCO have caused terrorist groups to significantly change their operational practices. Heightened security measures in most countries caused terrorist groups to establish relationships with other non-state actors, opening new doors of opportunity and "changes to the financing of many terrorist groups over the past couple of decades have brought about some convergence between insurgents and terrorist groups and organized crime networks, creating a potential indirect link between terrorism and organized piracy."[38] Al-Qaeda, for example, has long been interested in exploiting the soft targets of the maritime domain in order to disrupt the global market and use maritime trade routes for attacks.[39] Abdul Rahim Mohammed, al-Qaeda Chief of Naval Operations, captured by the United States in Yemen in 2002, stated that al-Qaeda intended to increase terrorist attacks against shipping.[40] Given the successful al-Qaeda attack on the USS *Cole* in Yemen Harbor in 2002, this threat should be taken seriously.

As Al Shabab and Islamic militants continue to gain strength in Somalia, increased cooperation with al-Qaeda appears plausible as it could extend the global reach of jihadists. Somali pirates already cooperate with Al Shabab, providing cuts from ransom money so Al Shabab can purchase weapons and finance operations as it pursues its goal of controlling Somalia. A significant difference between the ideology of Al Shabab and that of the CIC is Al Shabab supports terrorism and piracy and the CIC did not. In fact, the CIC sent two letters to the U.S. Government (USG) promising to be a responsible actor in the international community and would ensure Somalia did not become a safe haven or transit point for terrorists.[41] Therefore, it may be in the best interest of Somali pirates to continue cooperation with Al Shabab and exploit financial opportunities with other non-state actors, such as al-Qaeda or other terrorist groups.

Somali pirates can provide training to terrorist groups on the use of small boats, navigation at sea, and the tactics, techniques, and procedures used to hijack a large vessel. Somali pirates can also help terrorists in transporting weapons and munitions using a tactic demonstrated by the Palestinian Liberation Organization (PLO) in 2001. The PLO placed weapons, rockets, and munitions in water tight bags and packed them in barrels. The barrels were tied together and loaded onto a fishing vessel. Once at sea, the barrels were unloaded into the sea and then were picked up by smaller boats and transported into Gaza in Israel.[42] Somali pirates are well equipped to execute this technique to facilitate al-Qaeda or other terrorist groups in getting weapons into Somalia and other African nations for use in global terror operations.

Direct cooperation with terrorist groups is risky for Somali pirates as it will bring even greater international attention to their operations and they could then be identified as terrorists. Since the United States currently treats terrorism as a military vice law enforcement problem, the United States could then conceivably target Somali pirates like any other combatant.[43] Cooperation between Somali pirates and terrorists would allow the United States to address Somali pirates under OCO, committing significant resources to deter this threat. This may be a risk Somali pirates are willing to take if the financial gains outweigh the potential losses. However, formal cooperation is not required between pirates and terrorist groups for a relationship to be maintained.

Piracy and terrorist operations conducted simultaneously from Somalia can be used as a diversion and attempt to confuse international legal and military efforts to combat both activities. When the "multiple layers of criminal activity are in operation simultaneously in an underworld environment that is difficult for an outsider to penetrate, they can confuse the intelligence picture and make terror activities even harder to discern."[44] Al-Qaeda would benefit a great deal from this increased Clausewitzian fog as it is an organization without state sponsorship and requires conditions to reduce the signature of its operations. This mutually supporting indirect relationship would have less of an adverse affect on Somali pirates and allow them to practice business as usual. Under this scenario, it would be difficult to prove a linkage between the pirates and a terrorist organization, and the Somali pirates would keep their international status as criminals vice terrorists.

RECOMMENDATIONS

The solution to defeating Somali pirates starts ashore. The first step in preventing or deterring Somali pirates is to transform the Somali society and political architecture, and eliminate the conditions fueling piracy. Such transformation must come from Somali people themselves; however, it is clear that the TFG is incapable of providing the strategic leadership to transform this failed state.

This transformation will likely occur through the application of international elements of national power. The USG will need to define its strategic leadership role in this effort of securing a vital artery in the global economy.

The time has come for the USG to step out from behind the ghosts of the 18 U.S. soldiers killed in Task Force Ranger and the failed U.S. foreign policy in Somalia. A USG policy should address the conditions contributing to Somalia as a failed state and compliment efforts of the international community to stabilize the country. Piracy will continue to flourish as long as the Somali government cannot enforce rule of law, provide essential services, and increase economic opportunities to the population.

The security of world commerce passing through the Gulf of Aden is of national interest to the USG since the continued attacks on maritime commerce in this region have real potential to disrupt the global economy. Somali piracy is one part of a larger global piracy problem requiring a coordinated international effort to address the complex political, economic, and social issues enabling piracy.[45] Rather than adopt a policy specific to Somali pirates, the USG should pursue an integrated, international policy toward global piracy, taking into consideration local conditions that enable piracy such as geography, culture, governance, and economic development, to ensure consistency within the international community. The USG and international community must be able to effectively deal with failed states for if they are ignored "then their problems, whether they involve piracy, smuggling or terrorism, will affect their neighbors and the ships that pass their coasts."[46]

The USG, through an interagency approach, will have to continue to work with the leadership of the TFG, the African Union (AU), and the UN to help establish the conditions for Somalia's reform. The international goal should be to achieve an effective and legitimate government with appropriate law enforcement and security apparatus, and an infusion of targeted economic resources providing opportunities that will eventually persuade pirates to put down their weapons.[47] Implementation of the Djibouti Agreement should be used as a starting point. In absence of achieving this agreement, the USG should continue to support UN efforts to stabilize conditions in Somalia and maintain formal relations with the TFG.

Another complex issue facing the USG is the likelihood that the TFG will collapse, allowing the Islamic jihadists of Al Shabab to control Somalia and exercise a conservative form of Sharia Law mirroring that of the Taliban and al-Qaeda. This same form of Sharia Law was exercised by the CIC in 2006, and although denounced by human rights groups throughout the world, the CIC authority significantly reduced piracy operations with a zero tolerance policy. If Al Shabab controls Somalia and has the means to prevent piracy, would the USG be willing to acknowledge Al Shabab's legitimacy, provided Al Shabab denounced terrorism? As long as a Somali government comprised of Islamic fundamentalists did not support regional or transnational terrorism, then acknowledging the legitimacy of that government may be a plausible and acceptable solution to ending Somalia's status as a failed state.

The collective actions of nation states in combating Somali pirates are more likely to succeed than individual actions. The actions of the USG, AU, European Union (EU), North Atlantic Treaty Organization (NATO), and UN must be coordinated to ensure the collective efforts are mutually supporting and establish conditions for long-term success. One of the first issues the international community needs to address is the regulation of fishing in the territorial waters of Somalia and outlying international waters. Fishing vessels from Europe and Asia continue to fish within Somalia's territorial waters, making it difficult for Somali fisherman to prosper. This continues to influence many Somali fisherman to resort to piracy as an alternate, and arguably more lucrative, income.

The U.S Department of State (DOS) and U.S. Agency for International Development (USAID) will need to work closely with U.S. African Command (USAFRICOM) and lead USG efforts. The USG cannot view Somalia only through a military lens because doing so would ignore the social, political, and economic issues enabling piracy to flourish. Recent dialogue of the USG with the UN, requesting that the UN Security Council pass a resolution allowing nation states to pursue Somali pirates ashore, will only yield short-term success. Somalia's transformation will take a holistic USG approach in order to assist in rebuilding the political, economic, and security infrastructure needed in a nation state. This will become increasingly difficult due to resource limitations and continued requirements to support OCO, including USG efforts in Iraq and

Afghanistan, as well as the current global economic crisis. Taking action now, however, could save the United States resources and lives in the future.

As long as the TFG is recognized as the legitimate government of Somalia, AFRICOM will need to pursue an aggressive security engagement program with the TFG to bolster the effectiveness of Somali law enforcement and security forces. Mobile training teams in law enforcement and maritime security are needed to properly train Somali law enforcement in combating piracy operations. AFRICOM's efforts must be linked to and support overall USG objectives in Somalia as defined by the DOS.

Combined Task Force-150 (CTF-150), a coalition naval Task Force led by U.S. Central Command's (CENTCOM) 5th Fleet, provides limited security to commercial maritime traffic sailing the shipping lanes through the Gulf of Aden. The focus of CTF-150 is supporting the GWOT. However, CTF-150 does not have enough resources to address piracy operations full-time. CENTCOM recently established an additional coalition naval Task Force, CTF-151, to specifically conduct counter-piracy operations in the Gulf of Aden, allowing CTF-150 to focus on OCO operations. The standup of CTF-151 received broad support from NATO and the EU. An EU Task Force is also conducting counter-piracy operations under Operation Atlanta. In order for CTF-151 and the EU Task Force to be a viable deterrent against Somali pirates, governments providing resources to the Task Force need to be prepared to support until the conditions ashore enabling piracy are eliminated.

Commercial maritime traffic should be restricted to the Maritime Security Area established by CENTCOM and patrolled by CTF-151. Due to the vast expanse of the Gulf of Aden, it is impossible to completely eliminate piracy. Restricting the routes used by maritime traffic, however, will significantly reduce the chances for successful pirate attacks. The shipping industry must take stronger measures in training mariners to make crews less vulnerable to pirate attacks. Somali pirates avoid confrontation and have been repelled by crews using high pressure water hoses, small arms fire, and increasing ship speed.[48]

The international shipping industry should strongly consider contracting private security firms to provide armed security for vessels transiting the Gulf of Aden. Security personnel should be equipped with both lethal and non-lethal capabilities to defend against pirate attacks. This should be supported by the UN Security Council with universal Rules of Engagement approved. The UN would also need to address and establish guidelines governing jurisdictional issues of pirates apprehended by private security firms during attacks. The SUA Convention is a good starting point.

Finally, considering the strategic location of Somalia to one of the world's major shipping routes and the inability of the Somali government to secure its territorial waters from pirates, the UN should consider modifying the language defining piracy contained in the UNCLOS and adopt language similar to the IMB definition of piracy. This provides greater flexibility to the international community to respond to acts of piracy, especially within the territorial waters of a failed state as in the case of Somalia. UN Security Council Resolution (UNSCR) 1846 of December 3, 2008, allowed governments cooperating with the TFG to enter Somalia's territorial waters, for a period of 12 months, and use all means necessary in order to repress acts of piracy and armed robbery.[49] The temporary authorities authorized by UNSCR 1846 became permanent with the approval of UNSCR 1851 on December 16, 2008.[50] However, these resolutions are only applicable to Somalia and do not address the global nature of piracy.

All nations relying on maritime commerce through the Gulf of Aden should be concerned about the impunity with which Somali pirates operate. The pirates threaten the daily security of the world economy and the global reliance on maritime commerce to supply it. Furthermore, cooperation between terrorist organizations and Somali pirates is a potential threat not to be overlooked. Somali pirates will continue operations as long as the international community fails to establish measures for the "pirates to be apprehended, tried, and convicted, and punished for their crimes."[51] Somali pirates ushered in a new golden age of piracy. Unless the international community acts in concert to address piracy, these non-state actors will continue to undermine the security of the global commons at will. Edward "Black Beard" Teach would surely smile in approval.

Notes

[1]Although piracy is prevalent throughout the world, this study is limited to Somali pirates due to Somalia's strategic location to one of the world's busiest commercial shipping lanes and the conditions existing in Somalia as a failed state that enable piracy.

[2]Kimberly L. Thachuk and Sam J. Tangredi, "Transnational Threats and Maritime Responses," in *Globalization and Maritime Power,* ed. Sam J. Tangredi, (Washington DC: National Defense University Press, 2002), 57.

[3]Joshua Sinai, "Future Trends in Worldwide Maritime Terrorism," *The Quarterly Journal* Vol. III, No. 1 (March 2004): 49 and 63.

[4]United Nations Convention on the Law of the Sea of 1982, Article 101, 61, http://www.un.org//depts/los/convention_agreements/texts/unclos/unclos_e. pdf. Although the United States has not ratified this convention due to disagreement over Article 11 and provisions for deep sea mining, the United States does accept all other articles of the convention as binding customary international law. Secretary of State Clinton has indicated she will make ratifying the convention a priority.

[5]ICC International Maritime Bureau, *Piracy and Armed Robbery Against Ships: Report for the Period 1 January–30 June 2008*, London, July 2008, 4.

[6]Reconciling the numerous international definitions used to define piracy and terrorism is outside the scope of this study.

[7]Jeffrey Fleishman, "Egypt and Other Red Sea Nations Target Pirates," *Los Angeles Times*, November 21, 2008.

[8]1988 UN Convention for the Suppression of Unlawful Acts Against the Safety of Maritime Navigation, http://www.imo.org/Conventions/mainframe.asp ?topic_id=259&doc_id=686. Allows UN member state parties to the convention, in cooperation with the UN Secretary-General and IMO, to build judicial capacity for the successful prosecution of persons suspected of piracy or armed robbery at sea off. UN parties to this convention have authority to create criminal offenses, establish jurisdiction, and accept delivery of persons responsible for or suspected of piracy. The United States ratified the convention in 1994. The convention is applicable to persons suspected of maritime terrorism.

[9]Michael Richardson, "Somali Pirates Running Rampant: Vigilance at Sea," *Institute of Southeast Asia Studies*, October 4, 2008, http://www.iseas.edu.sg/viewpoint/mr4OCT08.pdf.

[10]Daniel Benjamin and Steven Simon, *The Age of Sacred Terror*, (New York, NY: Random House, 2002), 323.

[11]Donna J. Nincic, "Sea Lane Security and U.S. Maritime Trade: Chokepoints as Scarce Resources" in *Globalization and Maritime Power*, ed. Sam J. Tangredi, 143-170 (Washington DC: National Defense University Press, 2002), 158. This concern is also echoed by Captain Pottengal Mukundan, Director International Maritime Bureau, stating that the heightened level of violence and frequency of pirate attacks are the primary concerns of the shipping industry.

[12]Martin N. Murphy, *Contemporary Piracy and Maritime Terrorism: The Threat to*

International Security, (London: Routledge, 2007), 31.

[13]Stephanie Hanson and Eben Kaplan, "Somalia's Transitional Government," *Council on Foreign Relations*, May 12, 2008, 2, http://www.cfr.org/publication /12475/.

[14]Moises Naim, "It's the Illicit Economy, Stupid," *Foreign Policy*, Nov/Dec 2005, 95.

[15]Moises Naim, *Illicit: How Smugglers, Traffickers and Copycats are Hijacking the Global Economy* (New York: Doubleday, 2005), 264.

[16]Ellen Knichmeyer, "On A Vital Route, A Boom in Piracy," *Washington Post*, September 27, 2008.

[17]Joshua Sinai, "Future Trends in Worldwide Maritime Terrorism," *The Quarterly Journal* Vol. III, No. 1 (March 2004), 61.

[18]Roger Middleton, *Piracy in Somalia: Threatening Global Trade, Feeding Local Wars*, October 2008, 2, http://www.chatthamhouse.org.uk/files/12203_1008 piracysomalia.pdf.

[19]*International Maritime Organization*, http://www.imo.org.

[20]John W. Miller, "Piracy Spurs Threats to Shipping Costs," *The Wall Street Journal*, November 19, 2008.

[21]Peter Chalk, *The Maritime Dimension of International Security: Terrorism, Piracy, and Challenges for the United States*, (Arlington, VA: Rand Corporation, 2008), 5-6.

[22]"Unprecedented Rise in Piratical Attacks," *International Maritime Bureau*, October 24, 2008, http://www.icc-ccs.org/index.php?option=com_content&view =article&id=306:unprecedented-rise-in-piratical-attacks&catid=60:news &Itemid=51.

[23]US Central Command Daily Operations Brief on June 17, 2010.

[24]Kimberly L. Thachuk and Sam J. Tangredi, "Transnational Threats and Maritime Responses," in *Globalization and Maritime Power*, ed. Sam J. Tangredi, 57-78 (Washington DC: National Defense University Press, 2002), 59.

[25]Raissa Kasolowsky and Simon Webb, "Somali Pirates Seize Saudi Tanker Carrying $100 Million in Oil," *The Washington Post*, November 18, 2008.

[26]Martin N. Murphy, *Contemporary Piracy and Maritime Terrorism: The Threat to International Security* (London: Routledge, August 17, 2007), 19-20.

[27]Peter Chalk, *The Maritime Dimension of International Security: Terrorism, Piracy, and Challenges for the United States*, (Washington DC: Rand Project Air Force, 2008), xiv.

[28]United Nations Conference on Trade and Development, *Review of Maritime Transport 2008*, Geneva, 2008, 9, http://www.unctad.org/en/docs/rmt2008ch1 _en.pdf.

[29]Ibid., 6.

[30]Murphy, *Contemporary Piracy*, 20.

[31]John W. Miller, "Piracy Spurs Threats to Shipping Costs," *The Wall Street Journal*, November 19, 2008 and Sayyid Azim, "Pirate Attacks Drive Up The Cost Of Shipping," April 12, 2009, http://www.msnbc.msn.com/id/30180080.

[32]Mohamed Olad Hassan and Elizabeth Kennedy, "Somali Pirates Riches Turn Villages Into Boomtowns," *The Huffington Post*, November 20, 2008, 3,

http://www.huffingtonpost.com/2008/11/19/somali-pirates-riches-tur_n_144942.html.

[33]National Commission on Terrorist Attacks upon the United States, *The 9/11 Commission Report*, (Baton Rouge, LA: Claitor's Publishing Division, 2004), 366.

[34]Ibid., 58.

[35]Ibid., 97.

[36]Ibid., 48.

[37]Peter Clottey, "United States Designates Somalia's Al Shabab As A Terrorist Group," *Voice of America News*, March 19, 2008.

[38]Murphy, *Contemporary Piracy*, 40.

[39]Michael Richardson, "A Time Bomb for Global Trade: Maritime Related Terrorism in an Age of Weapons of Mass Destruction," *ISEAS*, February 2004, 2, http://www.iseas.edu.sg/viewpoint/mricsumfeb04.pdf.

[40]Ibid., 8.

[41]Michael A. Weinstein, "The Islamic Courts Union Opens a New Chapter In Somalia's Political History, Power and Interest News Report" June 19 2006, http://www.pinr.com/report.php?ac=view_report&report_id=512.

[42]Joshua Sinai, "Future Trends in Worldwide Maritime Terrorism," *The Quarterly Journal*, Vol. III, No. I (March 2004): 54.

[43]During the administration of President Clinton, the United States viewed terrorism under the lens of law enforcement. It remains to be seen whether President Obama will revert to the law enforcement model or not. However, the law enforcement model is more consistent with the European perspective and may receive more international support.

[44]Murphy, *Contemporary Piracy*, 85.

[45]Ian O. Lesser et al., *Countering the New Terrorism*, (Washington DC: Rand, 1999), 142.

[46]Murphy, *Contemporary Piracy*, 87.

[47]Ibid., 128.

[48]Jack A. Gottschalk and Brian P. Flanagan, *Jolly Roger With An Uzi*, (Annapolis, MD: Naval Institute Press, 2000), 132.

[49]UN Security Council Resolution 1846. The UN Security Council first authorized this extraordinary measure in June 2008 as UN Security Council Resolution 1814 for a period of six months. http://www.un.org/news/pres/docs/2008/sc9514.doc.htm.

[50]UN Security Council Resolution 1851. http:www.un.org/news/press/docs/2008/sc9541.doc.htm.

[51]Donna J. Nincic, "Sea Lane Security and U.S. Maritime Trade: Chokepoints as Scarce Resources," in *Globalization and Maritime Power,* ed. Sam J. Tangredi, 143-170 (Washington DC: National Defense University Press, 2002), 166.

Clausewitz's Trinity and Strategic Decision-Making

by Fritz W. Pfeiffer

ABSTRACT

Clausewitz's "trinity" has provided a coherent means to understand war since 1832. This chapter argues that Clausewitz's trinity is also an applicable and useful means to understand strategic decision-making because it illustrates the influential role of emotion and chance on the process. Such an understanding promises to help leaders frame strategic choices in the future more completely.

This chapter first presents the theoretical background of Clausewitz's trinity along with an analysis of the concept. The chapter then uses the concept as a means to analyze and better understand the U.S. decision to invade Iraq in 2003.

This analysis does not offer a simple explanation for the 2003 invasion decision, but it does sharpen an understanding of the range of influences which framed and influenced it. It indicates that the most influential factors on this decision process may have been those which decision-makers had the least control over. Chief among these were the attacks of 9/11. Framed by a complex interaction of emotion and chance in the wake of 9/11, U.S. leadership, as well as a majority of Congress and the U.S. public, ultimately came to see invasion as a strategically viable option.

INTRODUCTION

A foundational concept in *On War*, Carl von Clausewitz's "trinity" has provided a complex yet coherent means to understand war that has inspired much analysis, interpretation, and debate since 1832 when it was posthumously published. Some scholars have argued that the trinity is representative of Clausewitz's most mature and enduring thought on the subject of war.[1] Others, however, have argued that the concept lacks the universality needed to capture war's varying characteristics over history, or its appearance in an increasingly technologically-advanced world.[2]

Al-Qaeda's terrorist attacks in the United States on September 11, 2001, seemingly mark a new characteristic of war. In a new, spectacular, and horrific way, extremists used the instruments of a modern society to successfully kill U.S. civilians, destroy U.S. symbols, and inspire unfamiliar feelings of insecurity and uncertainty in significant portions of the U.S. population. The possibility of such attacks in the future, perhaps with weapons of mass destruction, has become the pressing security concern in the United States. These attacks impacted the perspective and approach of U.S. strategic leadership, leading to a change in the national defense strategy, a re-allocation of national resources, a change to the organization of the government, and adjustments to certain laws. They also influenced rationales for war, as witnessed by the U.S. invasion of Iraq in 2003.

The possibility of significant terror attacks within the United States promises to influence the nation's security decision-making for the foreseeable future. Nine years after the fall of the towers, the leaders of the major U.S. intelligence agencies have stated that another attack is "certain" and clear evidence of foiled or botched attacks within the United States certainly seems to support this unsettling prediction.[3] Making high-quality strategic decisions in this ambiguous, complex, and potentially emotional environment promises to be extremely challenging. It is also vitally important. This chapter argues that Clausewitz's trinity is an applicable and useful means to understand strategic decision-making in this environment because it illustrates the influential role of emotion and chance on the process. Such an understanding promises to help leaders frame strategic choices in the future more completely.

The following approach will be used in this argument. First, the theoretical background of Clausewitz's trinity will be presented. Next, the chapter will examine the U.S. decision to invade Iraq in 2003. Employing Clausewitz's concept as a means to frame this strategic choice, the case study will analyze how the United States, when confronted with terror attacks, chose to invade a state not specifically responsible for them. Implications and recommendations for policy makers and strategic leaders will conclude this chapter.

CLAUSEWITZ'S TRINITY EXPLAINED

In Book One, Chapter One of *On War*, Clausewitz outlined his unique conception of war as: a paradoxical trinity—composed of primordial violence, hatred and enmity, which are to be regarded as a blind natural force; of the play of chance and probability within which the creative spirit is free to roam; and of its element of subordination, as an instrument of policy, which makes it subject to reason alone.

The first of these three aspects mainly concerns the people; the second the commander and his army; the third the government. The passions that are to be kindled in war must already be inherent in the people; the scope which the play of the courage and talent will enjoy in the realm of probability and chance depends on the particular character of the commander and the army; but the political aims are the business of government alone.[4]

In the first paragraph, Clausewitz described a first trio of influences: 1) *violence, hatred,* and *enmity*, 2) *chance* and *probability*, and 3) *reason* and *policy*. In the following paragraph, he inferred a secondary trio of components, consisting of generalized elements of a state: 1) *the people*, 2) *the commander and his army*, and 3) *the government*.

In their well-known study of this passage, Christopher Bassford and Edward Villacres have correctly indentified the first trio of influences as what Clausewitz meant as his "trinity." Distilling Clausewitz's original meaning into the terms "emotion," "chance," and "policy," they have insightfully observed that the three influences can also be generally categorized into the "irrational," "non-rational," and "rational" forces that inform war's nature.[5] Because these terms and categories are faithful formulations of Clausewitz's trinity, they will be used throughout this chapter in addition to Clausewitz's original words.

Clausewitz's secondary trio of components is a social reification of his actual trinity with each secondary component generally associated with a particular primary influence. Antulio Echevarria has noted that while Clausewitz saw his primary trinity as objective and universal, the secondary trio, which Echevarria refers to as the "secondary trinity," was subjective, representing elements of a political body which may or may not be part of war at all times and contexts.[6] The term *secondary trinity* will be used to refer specifically to Clausewitz's secondary trio of components: the people, the commander and his army, and the government.

Clausewitz saw his trinity neither as a static concept, nor a geometric construct, implying fixed relationships and strength. For him, the existence, relative strength, and interaction of the primary influences were the keys to a better understanding of war's variety and complexity. First, each of the primary influences was at play in some amount and at any point in time. Second, their relative strength to one another would also impact war's process and appearance.[7] Highlighting this point, Clausewitz described the pull of his three primary influences on war's process like an "object suspended between three magnets."[8] This description clearly conveyed his emphasis on the constantly changing interaction between the primary influences with the phenomenon of war moving in response. Significant enmity and emotion would likely support significant war policy; ambitious war policy goals would likely require substantial emotion to sustain them. Minor emotional stirrings might support only minor war policy aims; limited war policy aims might demand correspondingly limited passions.[9]

While in his trinity Clausewitz's separates enmity and emotion from policy and reason, his emphasis on their interaction reveals that clearly separating them is difficult in reality. Investigating this aspect further, Ulrike Kleemeier has persuasively argued that Clausewitz saw human emotion in war not as subordinate to reason but rather as helping to form the foundations for being *able* to reason to some extent in a challenging, uncertain environment.[10] By emphasizing the interaction of the influences of his trinity, Clausewitz clearly reserved a significant place for the pull of emotion and enmity on the dictates of reason and policy.

Clausewitz's trinity also captured his philosophical view of war as a complex, specifically human, phenomenon. This supports its use in not only understanding war's nature, but also in helping to understand the human decisions made within war at varying levels of scale. The primary influences act on and through individual agents: a soldier, his commander, a strategic policymaker, or a citizen of a state. These influences aggregate through the organizations, governments, or states of which individuals are part. For Clausewitz, any human organization within the environment of war, state-centered or otherwise, would be subject to the interactive influence of emotion, chance, and reason.

Importantly, reason is located *within* the war process and environment, not *outside* of it. In this manner, Clausewitz's trinity offers a theoretical means to understand how emotion and chance influence war decision-making and policy. The concept offers a glimpse into how individuals and organizations make meaning of their environment and, therefore, casts light onto the range of influences that may impact the way strategic decisions are both framed and made. Never intended to provide *the* answer in war, the trinity instead offers a better understanding of the environment in which *possible* answers in war will be crafted, implemented, or adjusted.

A written depiction of Clausewitz's trinity, including the variety of references used thus far to capture the influences, can be seen in Figure 1. The subsequent case study will use these terms to refer to the various influences of the trinity as appropriate. The first terms in each box are Clausewitz's own; the terms beneath them are the Bassford and Villacres formulations.

THE TRINITY APPLIED: CASE STUDY OF 2003 U.S. IRAQ INVASION DECISION

On March 19, 2003, the United States led a coalition to invade Iraq. President George W. Bush's address to the nation provided his rationale for the decision—to remove Saddam Hussein's regime and prevent him from threatening the United States, its allies, and Iraq's neighbors, with weapons of mass destruction.[11] This case study will draw on the primary influences of Clausewitz's trin-

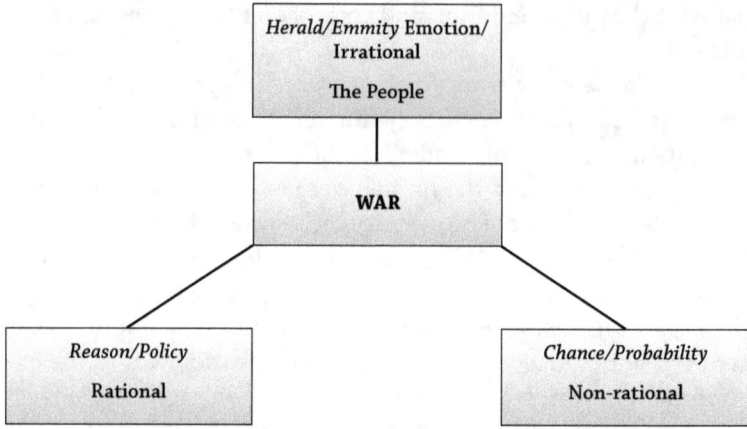

Figure 1: Clausewitz's Trinity. Clausewitz's terms are in italics; regular text terms are Bassford's and Villacres'.

ity to analyze and frame this strategic decision.

These primary influences may be observed using the following methodology. Reason and policy will be tracked through official U.S. policy at the time, along with content analysis of pertinent official, public statements of key U.S. leaders. Chance and probability will be detected in two different ways. The first will include those events and factors forming the context of the decision which were largely or completely outside the control of the U.S. government, including the actions of other agents. The second trace of this influence will consist of the actions of the U.S. military—the commander and his army in Clausewitz's terms—as it relates to forming the context of the overall decision. Enmity and emotion, the irrational influences, will be analyzed through public opinion polls, as well as other data that help to understand the mood and feeling of both the U.S. public, as well as key U.S. leaders.

Because Clausewitz saw the influences of the trinity as interactive and changing in time and space, this case study is structured to reflect this characteristic.[12] Instead of describing the influences individually across a wide range of time, their makeup and interaction will be presented and analyzed in two time periods. The first will be from the end of the 1991 Persian Gulf War to the terrorist attacks of September 11, 2001; the second will be from the aftermath of the 9/11 attacks to the 2003 invasion of Iraq itself.

FROM THE PERSIAN GULF WAR TO 9/11

REASON / POLICY / THE GOVERNMENT

After the expulsion of Iraqi forces from Kuwait in 1991 and throughout the rest of that decade, U.S. policy toward Iraq was marked by general hostility and relatively consistent confrontation. Following the war, a cease fire was established and the U.S. policy was to essentially contain Iraq. This policy was followed through the means of "no-fly" zones, U.N. sanctions, and occasional air strikes aimed at key Iraqi facilities. In 1998, amid concerns about Saddam's failure to comply with U.N. resolutions, the terms of the 1991 ceasefire, and his demonstrated abuse of his own citizens, the U.S. Congress passed the "Iraq Liberation Act" by a wide margin. This act formally codified U.S. policy toward Iraq as "to support efforts to remove the regime headed by Saddam Hussein from power ... and to promote the emergence of a democratic government to replace that regime."[13]

CHANCE / SKILL / THE COMMANDER AND HIS ARMY

Military operations toward Iraq reflected the general U.S. policy of containment even after the 1998 policy change. Designed to enforce the no-fly zones established after the 1991 war, Operation SOUTHERN WATCH constituted the significant, ongoing U.S. military involvement in the area. From 1992 to early 2001, pilots flew into the no-fly zone more than 150,000 times without casualty, and were engaged by either Iraqi radar systems or actual anti-aircraft weapons 500 times.[14] At certain points, and in response to specific or perceived Iraqi actions, military air engagement intensified. Following exposure of a plan to kill former President George H. W. Bush in 1993, U.S. forces struck Iraqi Intelligence Service facilities with tomahawk missiles. On the heels of the 1998 Iraqi Liberation Act, the U.S. government ordered a short, concerted air strike campaign against key Iraqi facilities named Operation DESERT FOX.[15]

Several significant terror attacks within the United States or against its interests abroad occurred during this period which are important to consider as part of this influence. The 1993 bombing of the World Trade Center, the 1995 Oklahoma City bombing, the 1996 bombing of Khobar Towers, the 1998 bombing of U.S. embassies in Tanzania and Kenya, and the 2000 attack against the USS *Cole* were the most significant. While the Oklahoma City bombing was attributed to U.S. extremists, all other attacks were tied to extremist cells operating in and around the Middle East. None of these attacks or the groups deemed responsible, however, was tied officially to Saddam Hussein during this period.

ENMITY / EMOTION/ THE PEOPLE

American public opinion reflected a feeling of relatively consistent hostility toward Saddam Hussein's Iraq throughout this period. In 1992, 55 percent of the American public favored sending U.S. ground forces to the area in order to remove Hussein from power. In 1993, this percentage spiked to 70 percent in the wake of the missile strike in response to the Iraqi Security Service's plot to assassinate former President George H. W. Bush. In February 2001, six months before the 9/11 attacks, this support percentage was back down to 52 percent.[16]

Despite the terror attacks mentioned above and any threat Saddam Hussein and his regime may have posed, the U.S. public had generally positive feelings about the course of their nation throughout this decade. During a time of economic prosperity, a record numbers of Americans felt secure and positive about state of the country and the direction it was going at the close of the 20th century.[17]

ANALYSIS AND EVALUATION

The influences of Clausewitz's trinity which could have supported significant ground action to force regime change in Iraq were present to some degree during this particular period. There was a government policy which could have directed such action; there was a level of enmity in the American public supporting military ground action; and there were events such as significant, publicized terror attacks and constant U.S. military operations that might have driven regime change. Yet the means the United States used to pursue its Iraq policy remained limited.

An understanding as to why may be drawn from considering the interaction and relative strength of the influences, not just their existence. While enmity toward Saddam's regime clearly existed, strategic leaders decided it was either insufficient for a more aggressive pursuit of policy, or that such a strategic choice was not a legitimate option in spite of the enmity that existed. It is also possible that, despite the multiple terror attacks during this period, none were of sufficient magnitude, impact, or clear attribution to Saddam's regime to dictate or inspire more aggressive action. In sum, the influences of the trinity did not lead U.S. decision-makers to frame the strategic environment in a manner where invasion occurred.

FROM 9/11 TO THE 2003 INVASION

On September 11, 2001, 19 extremists, supported by al-Qaeda, hijacked four commercial airliners and used them to kill nearly 3,000 people on America's home soil. Less than two years later, the United States invaded Iraq, even though Saddam Hussein's regime was not directly connected to this attack. An analysis of Clausewitz's influences and their interaction following the 9/11 attacks helps to better understand this result.

REASON / POLICY / THE GOVERNMENT

While the stated policy toward Iraq contained in the 1998 Iraq Liberation Act did not change in the wake of the 9/11 attacks, the degree and means by which it was pursued by the U.S. government altered significantly. In his first joint session address to Congress following the attacks on September 20, 2001, President Bush stated any nation harboring or supporting terrorism would be considered "hostile," and that the United States had a new bias for action in addressing security threats: "Either you are with us or with the terrorists" became de-facto government policy.[18]

Of note, Saddam Hussein and Iraq were not specifically mentioned in this address. Inside the government and outside of the public eye, however, the possibility of using a ground invasion in Iraq as a part of a larger strategy to protect the country was being considered almost immediately following the 9/11 attacks.[19] Following the military retreat of the Taliban from the major cities in Afghanistan in December 2001, the President did include Iraq publicly as a member of an "axis of evil" in his January 2002 State of the Union address and continued his argument for being more proactive in protecting the country.[20] This speech was viewed as "nothing short of a declaration of war" against Saddam Hussein's government.[21]

The U.S. government continued to stress its rationale for a possible invasion with Iraq, building upon these first policy statements. Published in July, the 2002 National Security Strategy presented a rationale for using military pre-emption to protect the country from regimes seeking weapons of mass destruction.[22] On September 12, 2002, the President argued for concrete and effective international action, stating that an Iraq led by Saddam Hussein was a "grave and gathering threat."[23] In the months leading up to the invasion itself, senior members of the administration continued to make the case that an invasion of Iraq to remove Saddam Hussein might be necessary to prevent weapons of mass destruction from being used to threaten the United States and the world.[24]

CHANCE / SKILL / THE COMMANDER AND HIS ARMY

Several events had significant impact on the strategic environment during this period that should be considered under this influence of the trinity. The most significant were the 9/11 attacks. Whether considered chance (an event beyond U.S. control), or enemy skill (operational success of al-Qaeda), these attacks demonstrated that the United States could be attacked in a significant, spectacular manner within its own borders and with great effect. With the country still trying to make sense of these attacks, and to determine its response, multiple letters carrying anthrax were mailed to several media centers and government office buildings. Five people were killed, precipitating the closure of U.S. Senate Office buildings and an adjustment of U.S. mail handling procedures.[25] In the space of just a few months, the U.S. public, heretofore feeling relatively positive about their country's well-being and security, experienced one spectacular attack that killed thousands, as well as another involving a biological agent delivered through their own mail system.

In response to the 9/11 attacks, U.S. military operations against al-Qaeda and the Taliban in Afghanistan commenced in early October 2001. By the end of November 2001, Northern Alliance forces, supported by U.S. military personnel, were in control of the major Afghan cities with Taliban forces retreating into the surrounding mountains. The skill and resources of U.S. and Northern Alliance forces, in combination with the quality of Taliban forces and a certain amount of luck, produced a quick and visible military success. This low-casualty success in Afghanistan, heretofore the "graveyard of Empires," contributed to the environment in which subsequent U.S. decisions about Iraq would be framed.

The role of intelligence, specifically the chance of its accuracy or inaccuracy, was another influence which framed U.S. decision-making during this period. Direct attribution for the 9/11 attacks was relatively straightforward. Other information was less clear, including responsibility for the anthrax mailings which remained an open case until 2010.[26] Intelligence connecting Saddam Hussein's regime to the 9/11 attackers surfaced, but a later Presidential Commission found no evidence to support this connection.[27] Intelligence widely believed to be accurate at the time indicating Saddam Hussein's weapons of mass destruction program was presented to U.S. leaders, the public, and the international community, but this information was later determined wrong as well.[28] Examining why intelligence can be wrong is beyond the scope of this study, but recognizing that the United States might frame strategic decisions on faulty intelligence is important.

ENMITY / EMOTION / THE PEOPLE

While there had been terrorist attacks within the United States before, none came close to registering with the same psychological impact on the U.S. public as the 9/11 attacks.[29] The sheer spectacle and horror of the attack, carried to every household with a television, changed the way many in the United States viewed the world and made them feel vulnerable and insecure within their own country. The real possibility of another attack loomed in the minds of both private citizens as well as policy makers.[30] The anthrax mailings immediately following added to this impact. Such feelings translated into action: statistics showed a significant increase in gun and ammunition sales in the three months following 9/11.[31]

U.S. public opinion polls reflected a sharp increase in enmity toward Saddam Hussein's regime in the immediate wake of the attacks as well. Polls taken in November 2001 showed that U.S. public support for a military ground operation to remove Saddam spiked to 74%—over 20% higher than just nine months prior.[32] This high level of support did not sustain itself, however. A year after the 9/11 attacks, it had moved back down to the high 50's where it stayed to a large extent all the way until the actual invasion itself. According to several polls, the next time support for military ground operations would be as high as it was immediately after 9/11 was actually *after* the invasion occurred.[33]

The U.S. House of Representatives reflected its constituencies' heightened enmity toward Saddam Hussein's regime as well. On October 16, 2002, the House passed the "Authorization for Use of Force Against Iraq Resolution" with strong majority of 68%, actually exceeding the percentage of general public support for this option at the time by a considerable margin.[34]

The 9/11 attacks and the environment of insecurity following them inspired a level of enmity and emotion directed toward Saddam Hussein in the minds of individual strategic leaders as well. President Bush acknowledged that the attacks changed his personal view of the world, and his view of the threat of Saddam Hussein, in rational as well as emotional ways.[35] The rhetorical wording of the 2002 State of the Union, as well as other public statements, further reflected the President's personal enmity toward not only those responsible for terror, but Saddam Hussein himself. The Vice President also held significant and passionate feelings about the threat of Saddam following the attacks.[36] In his autobiography, *American Soldier*, General Tommy Franks recalled that upon hearing about the anthrax attacks in October 2001, he immediately thought of the significant threat that Saddam posed to the United States and the world.[37] When asked about doubts as to Saddam's possession of weapons of mass destruction, National Security Advisor Rice may have accurately captured the feelings of many in U.S. leadership circles saying, "We don't want the smoking gun to be a mushroom cloud."[38] Her statement at the same time expressed a genuine and passionate concern by some within the Bush administration for the threat posed by Saddam Hussein after 9/11 to U.S. national security.

ANALYSIS AND EVALUATION

Some analysts have argued that the decision to invade Iraq in 2003 was a result of being led to war by a few members of the U.S. government.[39] Other scholars have maintained that the government used rhetoric to inspire unprecedented public support for the Iraq invasion by connecting Saddam with 9/11 in public statements.[40] While such arguments have some basis, this analysis using the trinity indicates they may also be over-simplifying and not accounting for a wider range of influences which framed and informed the environment. The war process required more than just government leadership; it required significant emotion and enmity as well. U.S. public support for ground operations to remove Saddam spiked at its highest level in the months immediately following 9/11, *prior* to any significant levels of government rhetoric drawing a public connection between 9/11 and Saddam. In other words, there was a significant outpouring of enmity in the U.S. public, born out of the attack by al-Qaeda, yet also directed toward Saddam Hussein without much involvement by the government at all.

This analysis strongly indicates that the most influential aspects of Clausewitz's trinity on this decision process may have been those which were not easily averted or controlled. Chief among these were the 9/11 attacks. These attacks, in conjunction with the anthrax attacks, significantly increased feelings of insecurity and emotion in the minds of the U.S. public and its national leaders. While this heightened enmity was certainly directed toward the perpetrators and supporters of these attacks, it also transferred measurably and immediately toward Saddam Hussein's regime as well. Pushed by heightened emotion and the press of uncertainty following 9/11, strategic leaders, as well as the U.S. public, began to see a compelling reason for a more aggressive policy toward Iraq. Quick, low-cost military success in Afghanistan, uncertainty about U.S. domestic security, and contemporary certainty of the accuracy of crucial intelligence, continued to feed the interaction of emotion and reason. This injected more uncertainty, more emotion, and a stronger bias for action into an already volatile environment.

The attacks of 9/11 spawned significant emotional stirrings in the minds of many, leading them to view an invasion of Iraq as an increasingly viable strategic option. Framed by a continuing interaction of emotion and chance in the wake of 9/11, many U.S. leaders, as well as a majority of Congress and the U.S. public, came to see this option as the only one.

IMPLICATIONS AND RECOMMENDATIONS

This use of Clausewitz's trinity to better understand the U.S. decision to invade Iraq in 2003 does not offer a simple explanation, a definitive answer, or a clear future strategic course. It does, however, illuminate how an interaction of emotion and chance served to frame strategic choice. There are several important implications for U.S. strategic leaders which can be derived from this conclusion.

The Strategy of Terror: Know the Enemy. This analysis indicates that agents can use spectacular, high-casualty, terrorist attacks within the United States to provoke significant U.S. military action against entities not necessarily responsible for them. By provoking enmity and emotion, users of terror can seek to leverage the irrational influences of the trinity to inform and guide reason, thereby influencing U.S. national policy and strategy. While terrorists attacks may be thought of as targeting public opinion to produce results, this study indicates that such an attack could be effectively used to influence a senior strategic leader's decision-making process.

The Effect of Terror on U. S. Institutions: Know Your State. While some have expressed concerns about a democratic public's inability to control its passions, thus leading to poor, collective decisions, this analysis indicates this concern may not be entirely accurate. Significant terror attacks, like those of 9/11, will clearly and immediately impact the emotions and the decision-making tendencies of individuals. But when aggregated into larger groups, like the components of the state, this impact tended to attenuate rather than build in this case study. While strategic leaders may feel compelled to respond quickly and decisively to match the short-term emotions and opinions of the larger public, this analysis indicates that there is time in which to make decisions.

The Strategic Leader: Know Yourself. This study strongly indicates that effective strategic decision-making is at root a deliberative act of self-control: an internal effort to recognize the power of emotion in thought, identify its cause, and place it in proper balance. In an environment of crisis, this is especially difficult. It is also the time when it is most important. Terrorist attacks target the decision-making of individuals by leveraging emotional influences to goad one's reason to follow a particular course of action. Deliberative efforts to recognize this play on emotion and mitigate it must be part of the strategic leader's decision-making process, just as they might seek to recognize other types of bias in their thought.

The potential impact of emotion on decision-making in such a moment of crisis underscores the need for strategic leaders to show policy restraint immediately following such an attack. Attribution for the attacks promises to be difficult, even inconclusive or conflicting. Initial restraint recognizes this characteristic of the environment and allows room for more options and alternative strategies in the future. Such restraint is not a sign of weakness or passivity, although such charges should be anticipated. It instead reflects first an awareness of self, an awareness of the nation's characteristics, and an awareness of the potential designs of some adversaries.

Finally, this analysis illustrates that Clausewitz's trinity can help one better understand the environment in which strategic problems are framed, as well as how strategic decisions are made. Clausewitz's thought has long been part of the curriculum at U.S. Professional Military Education (PME) institutions as a means to understand war. This chapter illustrates that it has specific utility as a means to understand how strategic leaders view the challenges facing them. U.S. PME schools should present his concept, not only as a foundational means to understand war, but also specifically as a means to understand strategic decision-making within conflict. In this way, the aggregate chance of emotion *sustaining* pragmatic decision-making, rather than unconsciously *guiding* it, can be increased.

THE PLAY OF EMOTION, CHANCE, AND REASON ON STRATEGIC DECISIONS

This chapter used Clausewitz's trinity as a means to better understand the U.S. decision to invade Iraq in 2003, hoping to gather useful insight and support future strategic decision-making. Seeking to reflect the basic objectivity of the trinity itself, it has deliberately tried to avoid evaluating whether the decision was "good" or "bad," "just" or "unjust." Instead, it has illustrated that the decision was a process, influenced and framed by a complex interaction of emotion, chance, and reason at varying levels. It has also highlighted the inherent difficulties of clearly separating emotion from reason in the strategic decision-making process due to the complexity and fluidity of their interaction. In war, as well as in war-decisions, emotion and reason are intertwined and conflated in a manner which makes it difficult to consider them in isolation from one another. Clausewitz's trinity offers not only a thorough means for U.S. strategic leaders to understand war's nature, but also a useful way to better understand how they may view problems and then make decisions. In an increasingly complex and uncertain strategic environment, such an understanding is critically important.

Notes

[1]Bassford (2007) and Echevarria (2007).

[2]Martin Van Crevald (1991) and John Keegan (1993).

[3]"Intelligence Chiefs Say Another Terror Attempt in U.S. is 'Certain'", *CNN*, February 3, 2010, http://www.cnn.com/2010/POLITICS/02/02/us.terror.attacks/index.html (February 10, 2010).

[4]Carl von Clausewitz, *On War*, ed. Michael Howard and Peter Paret, trans. Michael Howard and Peter Paret (Princeton, NJ: Princeton University Press, 1976), 89.

[5]Christopher Bassford and Edward J. Villacres, "Reclaiming the Clausewitzian Trinity," *Parameters* 25, no. 3, (Autumn 1995): 16.

[6]Antulio J. Echevarria II, *Clausewitz and Contemporary War* (New York: Oxford University Press 2007), 73.

[7]Clausewitz, 88.

[8]Ibid., 89.

[9]Ibid., 88.

[10]Ulrike Kleemeier, "Moral Forces in War" in *Clausewitz in the 21st Century,* ed. by Hew Strachan and Andreas Herberg-Rothe (New York: Oxford University Press, 2007), 108.

[11]George W. Bush, "Address to the American People," *CNN*, March 19, 2003, http://www.cnn.com/2003/US/03/19/sprj.irq.int.bush.transcript (January 5, 2010).

[12]Because the three variables of the concept are highly correlated to one another, any analysis using Clausewitz's trinity poses an unavoidable challenge of multicollinearity. This makes definitively identifying causality difficult. This characteristic makes clearly attributing data like public statements of U.S. officials to only one influence equally difficult. For example, public statements by key U.S. leaders could be thought of as influenced by both the emotion of the moment as well as by more reasoned estimation. In the end, this challenge is unavoidable and should encourage the reader to consider the complexity and insightfulness of Clausewitz's trinity as a whole, rather than as separate parts.

[13]*Iraq Liberation Act*, H.R. 4655, 105th Cong., (1998).

[14] "Operation Southern Watch," *Global Security*, http://www.globalsecurity.org/military/ops/southern_watch.htm (January 12, 2010).

[15]See "Operation DESERT FOX," *Department of Defense*, http://www .defense .gove/specials/desert_fox.

[16]Gallup Poll 1633, "Iraq," *Gallup*, http:www.gallup.com/pol/1633/Iraq.aspx (January 10, 2010).

[17]Gallup Poll 124787, "The Decade in Review: Four Key Trends", *Gallup*, December 29, 2009, http://www.gallup.com/poll/124787/decade-review-four-key-trends.aspx (January 9, 2010).

[18]George W. Bush, "Address to a Joint Session of Congress and the American People," *The White House*, September 20, 2001, http://georgebush-whitehouse .archives.gov (January 4, 2010).

[19]Douglas J. Feith, *War and Decision: Inside the Pentagon at the Dawn of the War on Terrorism* (New York: Harper Collins, 2008), 66-67.

[20]George W. Bush, "State of the Union Address," *The White House*, January 29, 2002, http://georgebush-whitehouse.archives.gov (January 4, 2010).

[21]Charles Krauthammer, "Redefining the War," *The Washington Post*, February 1, 2002.

[22]"The National Security Strategy of the United States 2002," *The White House*, September 17, 2002, http://georgebush-whitehouse.archives.gov (January 10, 2010).

[23]George W. Bush, "Address to the United Nations", *CNN*, September 12, 2002, http://archives.cnn.com/2002/US/09/12/bush.transcript (January 10, 2010).

[24]Feith (2008) argues that a 9/11 - Saddam Hussein connection was not necessary to justify invasion and clouded what he saw as the true rationale for such military action: self-defense (see pages 234, 262, 323). He clearly acknowledges that 9/11 made concerns about defending the country from Saddam Hussein more pressing and that given the potential impacts of future attacks with WMD, it would be irresponsible to leave him in power (see pages 233, 238, 504).

[25]"Amerithax Fact Sheet," *Federal Bureau of Investigation*, September 2006, http:///fbi.gov/anthrax/amerithaxlinks.htm (January 13, 2010).

[26]"FBI Concludes Investigation in 2001 Anthrax Mailings," *CNN*, February 19, 2010, http://www.cnn.com/2010/CRIME/02/19/fbi.anthrax.report/index.html (March 17, 2010).

[27]*Final Report of the National Commission on Terrorist Attacks Upon the United States* (Washington DC: GPO, 2004), 66.

[28]"Transcript of Powell's U.N. Presentation," *CNN*, February 6, 2003, http://www.cnn.com/2003/US/02/05/sprj.irq.powell.transcript (February 19, 2010). See also *The Commission on the Intelligence Capabilities of the United States Regarding Weapons of Mass Destruction* (Washington DC: GPO, 2002), 3.

[29]Howard J. Stein, "Days of Awe: September 11, 2001 and its Cultural Psychodynamics", *Journal for the Psychoanalysis of Culture and Society*, 8, no.2 (Fall 2003): 187-188.

[30]Gallup Poll 4909, "Terrorism in the United States" where upwards of 80-90% of the public believed another attack inside America was at least "somewhat likely" for sustained periods of time. Also Feith, 121.

[31]Al Baker, "A Nation Challenged: Steep Rise in Gun Sales Reflects Post-Attack Fears", *New York Times*, December 16, 2001, http://www.nytimes.com/2001/12/16/nyregion/nation-challenged-personal-security-steep-rise-gun-sales-reflects-post-attack.html?pagewanted=3 (January 10, 2010).

[32]Gallup Poll 1633.

[33]Ibid.

[34]*Authorization for Use of Force Against Iraq Resolution*, Public Law 107-243-Oct.16, 2002, http://www.c-span.org/Content/PDF/hjres114.pdf (January 17, 2010).

[35]Bob Woodward, *Plan of Attack* (New York: Simon & Schuster, 2004), 24-27.

[36]Woodward, 3, 175, 292.

[37]Tommy Franks, *American Soldier* (New York: Harper Collins, 2004), 268.

[38]"Top Bush Officials Push Case Against Saddam", *CNN*, September 8, 2002, http://archives.cnn.com/2002/ALLPOLITICS/09/08/iraq.debate (January 4, 2010).

[39]See Haas (2009), Woodward (2003).

[40]Amy Gershkoff and Shana Kushner, "Shaping Public Opinion: The 9/11- Iraq Connection in the Bush Administration's Rhetoric," *Perspectives on Politics* 3, no 3 (September 2005): 525, http://www.jstor.org/stable/3689022.

The Case for a National Risk Communications Strategy for Mitigating Terrorist Attacks

by Roger R. Laferriere

ABSTRACT

This chapter argues for a National Risk Communication Strategy to reduce the indirect consequences of a terrorist attack. Death, injuries, and/or illnesses are among the obvious direct consequences of a terrorist event. There are also direct economic costs, such as the loss of property. These direct consequences are difficult to minimize because terrorist attacks are normally sudden and unexpected.

There are also many indirect, or secondary, consequences as a result of an attack, such as regional and/or national economic impacts. The 9/11 attacks are an excellent example of these second-order effects. Negative changes in social behavior occurred in the wake of this tragic event, such as the public's heightened fear of flying, which resulted in increased traffic fatalities as millions took to the highways instead of the air. In addition, there was general increased anxiety across the United States that resulted in additional substantial medical costs. These secondary consequences are more manageable because there is time to address them. It is in the government's and the people's best interest to minimize the impact and severity of these secondary consequences. This can be accomplished by ensuring that the government and people react appropriately to actual, rather than imagined, risks. Effective risk communications is the means to accomplish this end.

Additionally, community resilience following a terrorist attack is important for enabling residents to continue their way of life and minimize secondary consequences. A community that rapidly recovers also sends a message to the terrorists that it will not submit to fear. However, communities will not resume their normal way of life unless they understand the risks and how to safeguard against them. Therefore, risk communications is enormously important in building and sustaining community resilience.

The evidence is very strong that proper risk communications reduces the negative consequences of any event, terrorism or otherwise. While risk communications plans exist at a handful of agencies, the federal government has not adopted a government-wide national risk communications approach to terrorist attacks. Instead, its communication approach during an incident has tended to be one-way: from the government to the people, leaving little in the way of collaboration and trust between the two. Additionally, those government agencies with risk communication programs do not coordinate amongst themselves or down to state and local levels, therefore risking the potential for communicating conflicting messages during a real incident. Such a poor approach has and will continue to add unintended consequences, inhibit community resilience, and impose enormous unnecessary costs on society.

What is needed now from the national leadership is to institutionalize risk communications throughout the country. This is best accomplished by developing a National Risk Communications Strategy for terrorist events. If the government leadership does not effectively communicate risks to the public, prior to, during, and following a terrorist attack, they are likely to dramatically exacerbate unintended consequences. In essence, they will be aiding the terrorists in accomplishing their goals.

I know no safe depository of the ultimate powers of society but the people themselves; and if we think them not enlightened enough to exercise their control with a wholesome discretion, the remedy is not to take it from them, but to inform their discretion by education. This is the true corrective of abuses of constitutional power.
—*Thomas Jefferson in a letter to William Charles Jarvis, September 28, 1820*

THE PROBLEM WITH IGNORING THE BOTTOM OF THE ICEBERG

The goal of a terrorist, according to the U.S. Federal Bureau of Investigation (FBI), is to commit "a violent act or an act dangerous to human life, in violation of the criminal laws of the United States, or of any state, to intimidate or coerce a government, the civilian population, or any segment thereof, in furtherance of political or social objectives."[1] Coercion and intimidation are accomplished by creating fear through horrific acts of violence, such as mass murder, assassination, and kidnapping. Fear is the terrorist's force multiplier; it can create increased anxiety, panic, and depression, as well as exacerbate the immediate consequences of a terrorist attack. These immediate consequences include death, injury, illness, fire, explosion, and pollution, among others. The secondary consequences of a terrorist attack, many of which are generated by fear, include psychological injury and economic damage not directly caused by the attack itself. These secondary consequences can be prolonged, affect a much broader segment of the population and, in some cases, result in much higher costs (primarily economic) than those stemming from an event's immediate impact. In any terrorist attack, the immediate costs are just the tip of the iceberg. Below the surface lies the behemoth of secondary costs.

To minimize secondary costs, strong community resilience must be built. Community resilience is the community's ability to recover from a terrorist attack. Quick recovery means resuming a community's way of life rapidly, thus minimizing secondary consequences and thwarting a key aim of terrorism. The best way to avoid severe secondary consequences and promote community resilience is to inform the public of the post-incident risks and how to safeguard against them. The process of communicating risks is called *risk communications*.

Unfortunately, U.S. risk communication (RISKCOMMS) programs are currently being implemented only in a handful of government agencies, mostly at the federal level. Moreover, little or no coordination has occurred between these agencies and those below them at the state and local levels, making the potential for conflicting messages and a loss of government credibility not just possible, but probable. Given this potentially dangerous situation, the Obama administration should prioritize the creation of a National Risk Communications Strategy for all levels of government to promote strong community resilience and reduce the secondary consequences of a terrorist attack. A National Risk Communications Strategy should take the form of a national document similar to the National Homeland Security Strategy or National Information Strategy signed by President G. W. Bush during his administration.[2] Developing and implementing such a strategy will greatly enhance the U.S. government's effectiveness in defeating the terrorists' goal of manipulation by fear.

ORIGIN AND EVOLUTION OF RISK COMMUNICATIONS

There is no universally agreed upon definition of risk communications. For the purposes of this chapter, however, the following definition, adapted from the National Resource Council, is used: "Risk Communication is an interactive process of exchanging *risk* information between governments, private institutions, and the public to achieve the mutual goal of minimizing adverse consequences to human health and welfare."[3] The key words here are "interactive" and "mutual," which point to the important roles played by all elements of society—government, the private sector and the general public—in effective risk communications. Dr. Vincent Covello, an expert on RISKCOMMS and founder of the Center for Risk Communications in New York, argues that the collaborative and participatory nature of RISKCOMMS is what distinguishes it from normal public relations.[4] RISKCOMMS, therefore, is as much about building relationships as it is about communications.

RISKCOMMS was developed in the 1970s when it became clear that governments and private institutions were finding it extremely difficult to convey pollution and health risks to the general public in terms they could readily understand. Soon, experts like Covello, as well as Dr. Baruch Fischoff, Professor of Social and Decision Sciences and Engineering and Public Policy at Howard Heinz University, and Dr. Peter Sandman, a preeminent RISKCOMMS consultant, began to refine and improve RISKCOMMS processes. Their improvements ensured a public understanding of pollution and health risks, which avoided unnecessary secondary costs derived from public misperception.

In the last 40 years, the Environmental Protection Agency (EPA) has conducted 40,187 environmental assessments for major pollution threats to the United States, and has successfully employed RISKCOMMS to engage the public and, when appropriate, allay concern.[5] Like all good RISKCOMM programs, EPA collaborated with local environmental and public health authorities, as well as conducted regular public meetings to convey RISKCOMMS messages and, more importantly, to form a partnership of trust with local communities. The agency has a team of community outreach specialists that can augment the responding pollution remediation teams. This successful employment of effective RISKCOMMS has generated a substantial following both in academia and within other agencies.

The study of RISKCOMMS has grown considerably since its inception. For instance, several major universities, including Harvard, Yale, and King's College in London now teach RISKCOMMS. The National Center for Biotechnology Information of the U.S. National Institute of Health records over 1,300 academic papers on RISKCOMMS just for carcinogenic products, which suggests a strong interest in RISKCOMMS within academia.[6]

It is beyond the scope of this chapter to discuss RISKCOMMS processes in detail, but the basic model is focused on creating messages from a team of experts, and then testing those messages in a scientific manner on a cross-section of a specific target audience. The messages are then used in exercises, drills, and real situations, and are constantly reevaluated for their effectiveness. Although a tremendous oversimplification, this description generally captures how the process works. Having the right team of experts, as well as the right target audience, is paramount. For example, Fischoff recommends a team composed of subject matter experts, risk analysis experts, behavioral scientists, and public affairs specialists.[7]

As terrorism catapulted to the forefront of public concern

after 9/11, the same challenge of communicating complex scientific risks to the general public was faced by federal government agencies, many unused to RISKCOMMS processes. These agencies fell into the same trap of their environmental predecessors before the advent of RISKCOMMS. They relied on ineffective public affairs communication techniques. Indeed, contradictory government messages created confusion, anxiety, and doubt resulting in significant secondary costs.

THE SECONDARY CONSEQUENCES OF INEFFECTIVE COMMUNICATIONS

In general, the failure of good risk communications can have serious deleterious consequences, four of which Covello identifies: 1) the diversion of resources from other important problems; 2) the overshadowing of real risks by perceived risks; 3) unnecessary anxiety and worry; and 4) feelings of apathy and hopelessness.[8] Wiser and Balicer determined that the public's concern about risk can be exacerbated by unfamiliarity, the potential for damage, the sense of a loss of control, and general uncertainty, not to mention a lack of trust in government authorities.[9] When the public's concern over risk increases, there is a much greater likelihood that risk misperception will increase as well, which can generate greater secondary consequences. Unfortunately, Wiser and Balicer's factors are all inherent characteristics of the aftermath of a terrorist attack, which is why the effective use of RISKCOMMS by the government is absolutely necessary.

All of Covello's negative effects, as well as Wiser and Balicer's triggers for increased public concern, occurred in the wake of the 9/11 attacks and the incident at Three-Mile Island. Millions in public health funding, an example of Covello's first effect, were diverted after 9/11 from more common infectious disease programs to bioterrorism, even though millions more have died from the former.[10] And in the three months following the attacks, 1,018 more traffic fatalities occurred when people decided that driving was safer than flying—Covello's second effect of real risks taking a back seat to perceived risks.[11] An example of Covello's third effect (unnecessary anxiety and worry) is illustrated in the Three-Mile Island nuclear plant emergency of 1979. This is also a good example of how secondary consequences can be more psychological than physical. One study of that incident found evidence of an "evacuation shadow," where individuals evacuated miles outside the risk zone.[12] The study attributed this to conflicting messages from government authorities, which confused the public. The result was traffic congestion and delays in evacuating those in the risk zone, a reprise of which could be costly during a biological terrorist attack where preventing the spread of the agent is critical.

Covello's fourth effect (apathy and hopelessness) was evident following the 9/11 attacks. A nationwide survey of 3,496 adults (78 percent participation) was conducted on September 23rd, days after the 9/11 attacks. Two additional surveys were conducted two and then six months after the first one. The researchers found that a large number of those surveyed, living well outside New York, experienced disturbing levels of trauma-related symptoms, which required hospitalization and therapy.[13] Another study reported psychological trauma after 9/11 as far away as Italy, India, and Belgium.[14] A third reported panic attacks in 11 percent of New York City adults, amounting to over 700,000 people.[15] All these can be related to the phenomenon of "clinical hysteria," where people in distress in essence make themselves sick. This phenomenon is psychologically contagious, and has the same symptoms as a biological, chemical, and radiological agent: headache, vomiting, gastrointestinal distress, dizziness, and anxiety. This clinical hysteria can cause more health havoc than a disease itself, especially when it is difficult for health officials to determine if the symptoms are causes by a WMD agent, or from clinical hysteria. Effective RISKCOMMS is an excellent remedy for reducing the number of clinical hysteria cases.[16]

Because the public has the least understanding and perhaps the most misconceptions about chemical, biological, and radioactive agents, the secondary consequences from these types of events can be quite severe. During the Tokyo Sarin Subway Attacks of 1995, 5,510 people sought unnecessary medical care when only 12 persons died and 17 were critically injured.[17] An example of public overreaction to a radiation event occurred in Goiania, Brazil in 1987. Two people found a source of radioactive material in an abandoned medical building. As a result of the material's spread, four people died and 249 were contaminated. An astounding 112,000 people, however, reported for unnecessary medical treatment.[18] No evidence was found of any risk communications during these events. The National Council of Radiation Protection and Measurements, charted by Congress in 1964 to provide public information on radiation, produced a report on managing terrorist events one month after 9/11. The report asserted that the *number one* problem with a radiological attack is the psychological aspect of the event, with thousands of citizens unnecessarily streaming to hospitals, overwhelming hospital capacity.[19]

The best example of poor RISKCOMMS during a biological attack within the United States was the anthrax attacks of 2001. Those attacks claimed the lives of five people over a three-month period and contaminated 20 others.[20] The avoidable secondary consequences were staggering: over 30,000 people obtained unneeded prophylaxis.[21] Because the government was ineffective in communicating in a timely manner, the media was forced to find its own sources and, consequently, reported incorrect information. When the media incorrectly reported nasal swabbing as the preferred method of detection, thousands of concerned citizens requested this unnecessary procedure.[22] When ciproflaxin was reported as the drug of choice, the public requested this treatment even though the alternative, dioxycline, had a lower risk of side effects and cost less.[23] Additionally, over 120,000 lab samples were taken from the public, which quickly overwhelmed the nation's laboratory capacity.[24] The public overloaded government agencies with inquiries on the risks posed by anthrax; in one week alone during the event, 2,817 calls were made across nine states.[25]

During the anthrax incident, the U.S. government did not communicate uniformly—different agencies and government officials offered conflicting messages. For example, President Bush advised Americans to continue with their normal routines at the same time that the CDC was issuing statements on necessary precautions to take.[26] A U.S. Army expert on biological weapons reported that the anthrax was "weaponized" without any clarification. The public perceived this as suggesting that the attack originated from a foreign terrorist source. The Army then retracted its statement and declared that the anthrax was "professionally" made and "energized."[27] This increased public confusion and reduced government credibility. Meanwhile, the Secretary of Human Health and Services (DHHS) commented that the first victim likely contracted the anthrax from a stream, which was grossly incorrect.[28] And the Attorney General speculated that the anthrax might be part of a terrorist attack.[29] Speculation is a bad technique for communicating risks. In all fairness to CDC and DHHS, they have made great strides in improving RISKCOMMS within their agencies since then. When considering all other federal agencies, however, they are the exception rather than the rule, and at the end of the day, the individual agencies' RISKCOMMS need to be coordinated to be effective.

THE RELATIONSHIP BETWEEN GOVERNMENT/PUBLIC TRUST AND RISK COMMUNICATIONS

RISKCOMM analysts have identified community resilience as a key element in defeating terrorist aims. The Gilmore commission, an advisory panel setup by the Bush Administration to assess domestic capabilities for terrorism involving WMD attacks, rightly points out that "communities defeat terrorism, not governments."[30] Effective RISKCOMMS can play a vital role in building community resilience, and community resilience is about creating a effective partnership between the government and the public.[31] Many argue that this partnership is paramount and must be one of the top priorities following a terrorist incident.[32] RISKCOMMS plays a critical role in engendering trust between the government and the public, another argument for instituting it nationally. The U.S. public's trust in the federal government during an emergency will quickly dissolve if the government is not effective in communicating risk. Unfortunately, many government authorities tend to degrade rather than build public trust, largely because the public is viewed as a major part of the incident rather than a partner.[33] By prescribing to this notion, governments erode confidence and undervalue the public's potential contributions.

RISKCOMM experts, however, take the opposite view— that during a major crisis, the public tends to be more cooperative and helpful than a hindrance.[34] During the Tokyo Subway Sarin Attacks of 1995 and the Bali Bombings of 2002, for example, the public was first on-scene and assisted injured members to the hospital.[35] Following the 9/11 attacks and Hurricane Katrina in 2006, the U.S. citizens converged to both incidents in the thousands with the best intentions of helping out. Rather than ignoring or preventing this natural inclination, the government should engage the public to leverage their support and, more importantly, to ensure their safety from incident hazards.

During a major pandemic event, terrorist introduced or otherwise, close cooperation between the government and the public is absolutely necessary to prevent the spread of the disease. The government must effectively communicate quarantine, personal hygiene, and prophylaxis precautions to avoid population devastation. The 1918 Flu Pandemic cost over 500,000 American deaths.[36] In modern times, where populations are much denser and public interaction much greater, a pandemic outbreak could be catastrophic unless government and public cooperation is effective.

Confidence in the government's management of an incident or crisis can quickly decline if the government mishandles its communications. The communication confusion during the anthrax attacks of 2001 is an excellent example. Despite the fact that the president was riding an enormously high approval rating following the 9/11 attacks (92 percent), the American public's confidence in the government's management of the anthrax attacks of 2001 suffered a severe blow.[37] Two separate polls conducted over the period of the event showed significant decreases in confidence (6-16 percent), in the government's management of the event.[38] Ironically, the president's own approval rating did not drop significantly, indicating lost confidence in the federal government but not in the President. Historically, the U.S. public turns first to Congress as the scapegoat for the nation's troubles, which is one reason why their approval ratings are generally lower than that of the president.[39] Good RISKCOMMS could have bolstered citizen confidence for both the Congress and the President.

During an incident, governments tend to withhold information to avoid creating undue alarm, which weakens trust between government and the public. By "restraining information about risk, they [governments] fail to recognize that they are undermining their own credibility," contends one researcher.[40] Department of Homeland Security Secretary Janet Napolitano stated that the Obama administration understands that the importance of the private-public partnership: "For too long we've treated the public as a liability to be protected rather than an asset in our nation's collective security. And this approach, unfortunately, has allowed confusion, anxiety and fear to linger."[41] That said, governments must also be careful about the timing and frequency of their communications. Governments that warn excessively will be the victim of the "boy who cried wolf" syndrome, while those that do not ring the alarm enough will be declared negligent.[42] This is why communications must be deliberate, planned, and continuously monitored for effectiveness.

Risk Communications in Existing National Strategy Documents, Plans, and Organizations

Despite the efficacy of RISKCOMMS in minimizing secondary consequences and facilitating community resilience, the United States has not implemented a government-wide, national risk communications strategy. Current U.S. national security strategy documents suggest that the government would like to build capacity in order to better respond to a terrorist attack. For instance, President George W. Bush's National Security Strategy for Combating Terrorism discusses improving "public safety emergency communications," and providing "the public timely and accurate risk communication during a public health emergency."[43] President Obama's 2010 National Security Strategy calls for "strengthening our preparedness and resilience," identifying the nation's "best defenses against this threat are well informed and equipped families, local communities, and institutions." The National Security Strategy continues, "And the Federal Government, drawing on the expertise and resources from all relevant agencies, will clearly communicate our policies and intentions, listening to local concerns, tailoring policies to address regional concerns, and making clear that our diversity is part of our strength—not a source of division or insecurity."[44]

On October 18, 2008, President Bush signed Homeland Security Presidential Directive 21, focused on improving public health and medical preparedness.[45] The document has strong overtones of RISKCOMMS: one of the four components under the community resilience section concentrates on educating civic leaders, citizens, and families on terrorist threats to ensure they "are empowered to mitigate their own risk."[46] In sum, U.S. government policy shows glimmers of understanding the importance of RISKCOMMS, but strategy formulation lags behind this appreciation.

The DHS-drafted National Response Framework (NRF) is a national document that provides *principles, roles and structures* that organize the way the United States responds to an incident.[47] It is *not* a plan, but a guidance document for responding to incidents of national significance for all executive agencies. More detailed response plans are written using the NRF as a guide. Although there is no specific mention of RISKCOMMS, there are some principles that facilitate good RISKCOMMS. For example, there are provisions for unified messaging, rapid information dissemination, and a solid chain of command from the federal to the local government levels. The NRF also recommends the use of an interagency Joint Information Center (JIC) to communicate to the public that can be used to support message consistency. Additionally, the framework mentions a single electronic network, the Homeland Security Information Network (HSIN) that could be used to ensure consistent RISKCOMMS messaging and dissemination. The DHS Office of Public Affairs (OPA) has responsibility for communicating back-and-forth to the Homeland Security Council, which in turn communicates with the President. This demonstrates a fairly well established command and control structure to facilitate the execution of RISKCOMMS if and when needed.

A critical principle missing from the NRF framework is the government/public partnership. The NRF's communication principles reflect a one-way communication system from the government to the people. There is no feedback loop or process to allow for the public to obtain answers needed from the thousands and potentially millions (think pandemic) of inquiries made following a catastrophic terrorist attack. Additionally, the government/public partnership and risk communication messages must be forged before an incident happens. The JIC previously mentioned is only stood up when an incident occurs and is disestablished when an incident is over. It is important for the government/public relationship to exist before and after the incident so it is a living continuous partnership. Pre- and post-incident communication programs are beyond the scope of the NRF.

At the federal agency level, there are about a dozen organizations that have RISKCOMMS programs.[48] The most prominent for a chemical, biological, radiological, nuclear or explosives attack are CDC, the Agency for Toxic Disease Registry (ATSDR), the Department of Defense (DOD), and the EPA. EPA, CDC and ATSDR have done a commendable job of instituting RISKCOMMS, with the latter two agencies improving primarily as a result of lessons learned from the anthrax 2001 incident. All have developed manuals, handbooks, and on-line courses. CDC and ATSDR's parent organization, the Department of Human Health and Services (DHHS), has a Bioterrorism Command Center and sponsors a National Association of County and City Health Officials, which has the responsibility of finding ways to improve RISKCOMMS.[49] The CDC has developed pre-scripted RISKCOMMS messages to be used by federal, state, and local responders in the event of a terrorist incident. These were developed in concert with four universities and 55 focus groups from across the United States.[50] Other agencies have also made a concerted effort to develop a RISKCOMMS program. DHS, for example, has sponsored a national university consortium for improving community resilience and the U.S. Army Center for Health Promotion and Preventative Medicine website manages all DOD RISKCOMMS training and outreach for DOD units.[51]

The efforts of these agencies are commendable, but serious problems remain. A terrorist event is likely to be an incident of national significance, with ramifications touching nearly all federal agencies. It is hard to imagine any executive agency not involved in the response to the aftermath of a nuclear weapons attack, for example. Such an event would surely demand a "whole of government" response.

The first problem with extant RISKCOMMS programs is the lack of central coordination between involved federal agencies to ensure message consistency. The difficulties created by message inconsistency were demonstrated in the earlier 2001 anthrax example. Although CDC has developed a decent library of RISKCOMMS messages, there is no evidence that other agencies have such a library, or have a policy to adopt CDC's library as the certified collection of default messages. Secondly, several other departments and agencies likely to get involved in a terrorist event do not have RISKCOMMS programs. Examples include all agencies of the Department of Justice, (FBI, U.S. Marshals, U.S. Attorney), Department of Transportation, and the U.S. Congress, just to name a few. Third, programs are disseminated in a one-way fashion via the internet with no confirmation of their use by local response organizations, likely to be at the spear-point of a terrorist event. In other words, federal programs suffer from fragmentation, inconsistency, and a lack of integration both horizontally and vertically (with state and local governments). A National Strategy of Risk Communications promulgated by the President would ensure that all executive agencies followed the same RISKCOMMS doctrine and protocols and eliminate these problems.

RISK COMMUNICATION ABROAD

A review of RISKCOMMS outside the United States reveals some lessons supporting the development of a national RISKCOMMS strategy here in the United States. Previous British and Israel examples have shown the benefits of RISKCOMMS to community resilience, with Canada, Singapore, and the EU also making advances.

Israel has suffered a tremendous number of terrorist attacks and provides a useful model to examine further. One study, for example, indicated that over 50 percent of adolescent Israeli citizens have been exposed to terrorism, with 20 percent losing a relative.[52] Continued exposure to terrorist events has forced the government to adopt RISKCOMMS principles. In essence, the Israel Government had adopted an *informal* but effective program as a matter of community survival. The nation has set up Community Stress Prevention Centers (CSPC) that provide psychological and social support, including RISKCOMMS, to victims of terrorist events. The CSPCs have provided over 9,000 hours of training, much of which includes RISKCOMMS.[53] Teachers are taught RISKCOMMS to help their students cope. Israeli leaders are experts in RISKCOMMS; some, like Nachman Shai, founder of the first television network in Israel and Israel Defense Forces spokesperson, have been called the "valium of the nation."[54]

Dr. Peter Sandman argues that terrorism is intrinsically communication: "communication is the event."[55] He compliments

Israel for its effective risk communications program and for plac-
ing terrorism in the proper context of risk: "People are more likely
to die of car accidents than terrorist events and the culture understands this."[56] He explains that terrorism's goal is to disrupt a
society's way of life—its normal routine. Israel, he contends, does
a remarkable job of defeating this nefarious goal through rapid
recovery and reconstitution. For example, if a suicide bomber attacks a major business, police, army, religious, and municipal leaders converge to the site and begin the process of rebuilding and
restoring the damaged building as soon as possible.[57] According
to Sandman, "This act in itself is a non-verbal form of risk communication."[58] One might also describe it as an act of defiance
against the terrorists.

The United Kingdom (UK), familiar with terrorist attacks
from its conflict with the Irish Republican Army (IRA) and having
survived Nazi aerial bombings in WWII, also merits review. After
the 9/11 attacks, Britain passed the Civil Contingencies Act of
2004, which specifically mentions RISKCOMMS and requires
public participation in defining and prioritizing risks, accomplished through local government public meetings.[59]

RISKCOMMS experts in Great Britain elaborate on the
country's approach to terrorist events. Dr. Ragnar E. Lofstedt,
the Director of the King's Centre of Risk Management at King's
College in London, contends that British citizens understand the
importance of resuming their lives following a terrorist attack,
which was clearly demonstrated following the July 7, 2005, attacks on London's subway system. For the most part, citizens re-
sumed use of the transit system within a few days after repair.
This remarkable display of resilience, he contends, was due to
constant, appropriate use of RISKCOMMS by the government.[60]
Sir Ian Blain, Metropolitan Police Commissioner, quickly got on
the air and advised all citizens to "Go in, Stay in, Tune in."[61] This
simple but effective RISKCOMMS message was already pre-de-
signed by the government and included as part of local response
plans. Additionally, the police share a pager alert system with
many large and small businesses, which they used to keep the private sector informed of developments.[62]

Despite their excellent efforts, in its after action report,
the Greater London Authority recommended the development of

and adherence to more rigid hourly time schedules to keep the public informed.[63] This is not an indictment of the response's success, but rather evidence of Britain's conscientious effort to continually improve RISKCOMMS. One might argue that Israel and Great Britain have experienced a much greater number of terrorist incidents, which accounts for their more informed and responsive publics, but it would be a mistake to discount the important role of RISKCOMMS in these two countries' approach to dealing with national crises or terror-related events.[64]

Great Britain and Israel have had the most success with RISKCOMMS, yet other nations are moving forward in developing national programs. During the SARS outbreak of July 2003, Canada experienced significant RISKCOMMS challenges, and made errors similar to the ones the United States made during the anthrax attacks. Unlike their U.S. counterparts, the Canadians responded by developing a national crisis communication program that centralizes all government RISKCOMMS and mandates rapid dissemination of RISKCOMMS messages for public safety.[65] In Singapore, the Ministry of Defense has adopted "psychological defense" as one of five total Defense Systems of the Nation.[66] Psychological defense is Singapore's way of referring to community resilience, but on a national level. They have identified community resilience as a national priority, and RISKCOMMS is an important part of their strategy.[67] Following the U.S. anthrax attacks of 2001, the European Union established Anthrax-Euronet, an electronic communication system to rapidly disseminate RISKCOMMS messages and other information.[68] Additionally, the World Health Organization (WHO) has published a RISKCOMMS handbook available on-line for all nations to use.[69] Unfortunately, the WHO has yet to prove its RISKCOMMS effectiveness; its mishandling of the SARS disease did nothing to properly categorize the risk against many more common fatal diseases.[70]

In summary, some countries have made great strides in incorporating RISKCOMMS into their response policies as part of their national strategy. Both the Israeli and British programs have been developed out of necessity and, although informal, remain largely effective. Israel and the United Kingdom have developed a "culture" of RISKCOMMS horizontally across their government agencies and vertically down to the lowest municipality.

In the United States, the RISKCOMMS culture is found only in a handful of federal agencies and is centered only on the government aspect of the RISKCOMMS partnership. Fortunately, the United States has not been forced to develop RISKCOMMS out of necessity, but the RISKCOMMS culture must be created within the United States to achieve the successes of Britain and Israel. Governments by their nature make up for the absence of a necessity driver by institutionalizing new behavior through law or policy. This is another important reason why a National Risk Communications Strategy is necessary—to create a culture of RISKCOMMS within the United States.

KEY ELEMENTS OF A NATIONAL RISK COMMUNICATIONS STRATEGY

Political scientists and military strategists describe strategy by *ends, ways*, and *means*. The ends are the objectives, the ways are the methods for achieving the ends, and the means are the resources required to execute the strategy. This chapter focuses on the ends and ways primarily and only touches slightly on the means (resource issues). Establishing the means for a National Risk Communications Strategy is a subject for further study.

The RISKCOMMS national strategy should identify three primary ends: first, to minimize secondary consequences to avoid unnecessary costs in human lives, health and welfare, the economy, and the environment. The second end is to maximize community resilience to ensure rapid recovery from a terrorist attack. The third end is to strengthen government and public partnerships to improve the nation's preparedness, response, and recovery efforts to defeat terrorist aims. All of these can fall under a single overarching strategic objective best described by General Larry Welch (U.S. Air Force (retired)) in testimony before DHS on community resilience: "Preservation of the American Way of Life."[71]

The remaining key elements can be placed within two major categories: planning and programs. Planning is the *effort* to prepare *in advance* of a terrorist incident to achieve the strategy ends. Programs are the *tools* that are employed before, during, and after a terrorist incident to also meet the ends. Each will be examined in turn.

Former DHS Secretary Chertoff emphasized the importance of planning in a 2008 speech: "If there is one lesson that 7 years since 9/11 should have taught, it is that advance planning is the only way to respond to a major threat."[72] Planning provides an opportunity for government and the public to work closely together. A National Risk Communications Strategy (NRCS) document would require a new Federal Risk Communication Plan consistent with the NRF. It would mandate that all current state and local emergency response plans to be amended (attached) or augmented (separate plan) with a RISKCOMMS plan. The NRCS must emphasize the importance of government and public partnership occurring during all phases of planning from concept, development, testing, and approval. In order to address all subdivisions within a community, local emergency management planners must include grassroots members of the community: civil and ethnic leaders, volunteer organizations, business associations, churches, and other citizen groups.[73]

The NRCS must list the critical components of federal, state, and local plans. An example of key components includes:

♦   a library of pre-scripted advance RISKCOMMS messages, tailored to all subgroups in a community;

♦   a list of national, regional, and local authorities on terrorism and WMD agents;

♦   a list of pre-designated trained representatives for conveying RISKCOMMS messages;

♦   a list of RISKCOMMS message development teams for pre-incident, incident, and post-incident deployment;

♦   a system for the rapid dissemination of RISKCOMMS messages from all levels of government to the public; and

♦   a program for continuous review and improvement of RISKCOMMS messages and programs.

On the federal level, the NRCS document should require an update of the National Response Framework (NRF), specifically, the Public Affairs and ESF 15 Annexes. Since the NRF's main focus is the incident and not pre/post incident programs, the Annexes must be revised to address RISKCOMMS during an event and therefore include those elements of RISKCOMMS for *incident response* from the NRCS (see programs below). Additionally, provisions need to be added to the NRF that focus on bolstering rather than subsuming local capability. Allowing local and state communities to manage an incident on their own, to the fullest extent possible, improves local community bonds and strengthens resilience while correspondingly decreasing feelings of vulnerability.[74] In addition to the planning components list above, the NRCS must require consistency between the NRF and all federal, state, and local RISKCOMMS plans. This model already exists in the provisions of the National Contingency Plan regulations (Title 40, U.S. Code of Federal Regulations, Part 300), where oil and chemical pollution response plans must be aligned from federal to local levels. RISKCOMMS plans must be exercised regularly, like oil and chemical plans.[75] This should also be prescribed by the NRCS document.

The NRCS document should require all agencies involved in a terrorist event to contribute to the development and continuous modification of the Federal Risk Communications Plan. The overall lead agency for this effort must be DHS since they have primary responsibility for coordinating the nation's response to a terrorist event. The Homeland Security Council must be briefed on the RISKCOMMS sections of the plan routinely. The Council must also have the plan ready during an emergency to access key RISKCOMMS messages as early as possible in order to assist the President in a timely fashion to address national public concerns.

In addition to formulating plans, the NRCS document should prescribe a number of programs (tools) to help facilitate RISKCOMMS during and after an incident. One program that is absolutely necessary is the revision of the Homeland Security Alert System. The current system is insufficient for one main reason: it does not require the public to take any action; therefore, it does not foster government and public cooperation, and simply increases fear. DOD has specific procedures for increased terrorist threats (THREATCON), which actively engages subordinate commands and the DOD community to protect themselves and DOD installations.[76] A national program like THREATCON would be more effective than the existing alert system.

Another key program in an effective NRCS document is public education. Compared to Israel and Britain, the United States program is severely lacking. Using these two countries as excellent examples, the United States should use RISKCOMMS to rally the nation around a message of resilience.[77] The current U.S. system is indirect, using the internet medium, which requires the public to "pull" information. RISKCOMMS messages need to be pushed as well so there is reasonable assurance the message is received. The United States appears to be reluctant to push information for fear of unnecessarily raising public anxiety. Experts like Dr. Sandman and others have demonstrated that "precautionary advocacy" results in substantial avoidance of psychological impacts during and following an attack.[78] RISKCOMMS messages should be provided through television, public service messages, radio, and mass mailings to homes. Schools can teach children drills, issue school assignments, and hold discussion groups to increase awareness.[79] The Citizen Corps, launched by President Bush in 2002 for the purposes of strengthening a community's response to terrorism, is an excellent resource for integrating and promoting RISKCOMMS education.[80] Currently, the Citizen Corps has no concrete incentive to provide public education, let alone promote a RISKCOMMS program.

The NRCS strategy should require a Federal Risk Communications Center (FRCC). The FRCC would have the sole function of coordinating RISKCOMMS for the entire federal government, centralizing and coordinating public risk communications for a terrorist event. The FRCC should be collocated with the National Response Coordination Center (NRCC), which is responsible for coordinating federal government operations in response to a national incident.[81] Both centers need to be joined at the hip with the National Joint Information Center (NJIC) identified in the NRF. The difference between the NJIC and the FRCC is that the former deals exclusively with the media regarding facts and data specific to the incident while the latter is primarily concerned with communicating risk. The FRCC develops the RISKCOMMS messages and monitors their effectiveness while the NJIC is responsible for communicating the messages to the media and the public. When not responding to an event, the FRCC can be the prime provider of government-approved terrorist RISKCOMMS messages through the various mediums discussed above. It can produce the single authoritative website for the information consumer, and can be the prime venue for

RISKCOMMS conferences, seminars, and training.

The FRCC could fall under the primary direction of the DHS Office of Public Affairs, which has direct links with the President's Homeland Security Council.[82] RISKCOMMS experts, public affairs experts from government, industry and academia, social scientists, and terrorist experts should staff the FRCC. The FRCC can also house deployable expert RISKCOMMS teams to support local responders. The FRCC must also be staffed with a massive public answering service, consisting of hundreds of individuals who can surge into the center to answer the thousands of phone inquiries expected during a major event. Here the FRCC can be most helpful to the local responders by removing this burden and allowing them to focus on resolving the incident.

Although these steps would not require a tremendous amount of government resources, especially when compared to other line items in the government's budget, they would pay great dividends. When the NRCS planning and program elements are in place, the U.S. government will be in the best position it has ever been to preserve U.S. national integrity in the face of a terrorist attack.

RISK COMMUNICATION: ESSENTIAL FOR NATIONAL PRESERVATION

The goal of risk communications in a terrorist attack is the preservation of the American Way of Life, the means are the government and the people, and the way is through the development and implementation of an effective National Risk Communication Strategy. The first step requires leadership. The President and Congress must acknowledge that a partnership between the government and the public is long overdue. The nation's leaders must take the initiative and forge a covenant with the public to be communicative, helpful, and a trusted partner in times of a terrorist event. Such a strategy allows the United States to bolster the collective resolve of its government and people, as well as communicate back to the terrorist "that government *of the people, by the people, for the people* shall not perish from the earth."[83]

Notes

[1]Federal Bureau of Investigation Counterterrorism Division, *Terrorism 2002-2005* (Washington DC: FBI, 2006), v.

[2]National Security Council, *National Strategy for Combating Terrorism,* (Washington DC: The White House, September 2006), http://www.whitehouse .gov/nsc /nsct/2006/nsct2006.pdf; National Security Council, *National Strategy for Information Sharing,* (Washington DC: The White House, October 2007), http://www .whitehouse.gov/nsc/infosharing /index .html.

[3]National Research Council, *Improving Risk Communication* (Washington DC: National Academy Press, 1989), 21. The National Research Council definition is "Risk communication is an interactive process of exchange of information and opinion among individuals, groups and institutions." This definition is considered incomplete for the purposes of this chapter because of the lack of 'risk' mentioned in the definition and what risk communications is intended to achieve.

[4]Ibid., 4.

[5]"Environmental Progress," U.S. Environmental Protection Agency, *EPA,* February 12, 2009. http://www.epa.gov/earthday/history.htm (February 12, 2009).

[6]"PMC Results," *National Center for Biotechnology Information,* http://www.ncbi .nlm.nih.gov/pmc?term=carcinogenic%20risk%20communication.

[7]Baruch Fischoff, letter to Chairman of the Homeland Security Science and Technology Committee, June 16, 2006, 2.

[8]Vincent T. Covello, et al., *Effective Risk Communication: The Role and Responsibility of Government and Non-Government Organizations* (New York: Plenum Press, 1989), 73.

[9]Itay Wiser and Ran D. Balicer, "Introduction to Bioterrorism Risks," *Risk Assessment and Risk Communication Strategies in Bioterrorism Preparedness,* ed. Manfred S. Green et al., (Dodrecht, the Netherlands: Springer, 2007), 105.

[10]Amanda J. Ozin et al., "Anthrax-Euronet and Beyond–Research on High Risk Agents," *Risk Assessment and Risk Communication Strategies in Bioterrorism Preparedness,* ed. Manfred S. Green et al., (Dodrecht, the Netherlands: Springer, 2007), 125.

[11]B. D. DeGroat, *Roadway Deaths Up After 911 Due Largely to Local Driving,* (The University Record Online, Ann Arbor, MI: University of Michigan, November 2004), 1.

[12]Kathleen J. Tierney et al., eds., *Facing the Unexpected: Disaster Preparedness and Response in the United States* (Washington D.C: John Henry Press, 2001), 188.

[13]Roxanne Cohen Silver et al., "Nationwide Longitudinal Study of Psychological Responses to September 11," *Journal of the American Medical Association* 288, no. 10 (2002): 1235.

[14]Anne Speckhard, "Prevention Strategies and Promoting Psychological Resilience to Bioterrorism Through Communication," *Risk Assessment and Risk Communication Strategies in Bioterrorism Preparedness,* eds. Manfred S. Green et al., (Dodrecht, the Netherlands: Springer 2007), 146.

[15]J. A. Boscarino et al., "Mental Health Service Use 1 Year after the World Trade

Center Disaster, Implications for Mental Health Care," *General Hospital Psychiatry* 26 (2004), 356.

[16]Speckhard, "Prevention Strategies," 144.

[17]Yamashina S. Ohbu and A. N. Takasu, "Sarin Poisoning on Tokyo Subway," *South Medical Journal* 90, (1997): 587.

[18]The International Atomic Energy Agency, *The Radiological Accident in Goiania,* (Vienna, 1988), 11, 46.

[19]John W. Poston et al., *NCRP Report No. 138–Management of Terrorist Events Involving Radioactive Material,* (Bethseda, MD: National Council on Radiation Protection and Measurements, 2001) 151-152.

[20]C. Chess and L. Clarke, "Facilitation of Risk Communication During the Anthrax Attacks of 2001: The Organizational Backstory," *American Journal of Public Health* 97, no. 9, (2007): 1579.

[21]Ibid.

[22]Government Accountability Office, *Report to the Ranking Minority Member Committee on Government Affairs, U.S. Senate. Better Guidance is Needed to Improve Communication Should Anthrax Contamination Occur in the Future,* (Washington DC GAO Report GAO-3-316, 2003), 17.

[23]Ibid.

[24]Ibid., 27.

[25]Ibid., 18.

[26]Lee Clarke et al., "Speaking with One Voice: Risk Communication Lessons from the U.S. Anthrax Attacks," *Journal of Contingencies and Crisis Management,* 14, no. 3, (2006), 161.

[27]Mathew Weinstock, "Senators want Better Guidelines for Responding to Bioterrorism," *Government Executive,* 2001, http://www.govexec.com/story _page.cfm?filepath=/dailyfed/1001/103101w2.htm.

[28]Clarke, "One Voice," 162.

[29]Ibid.

[30]James S. Gilmore, *The Fifth Annual Report to the President and the Congress of the Advisory Panel to Assess the Domestic Response Capabilities for Terrorism Involving Weapons of Mass Destruction,* (Arlington, VA: Rand Corporation, 2003), 108.

[31]Defense Threat Reduction Agency, Federal Bureau of Investigation, U.S. Joint Forces Command, *Human Behavior and WMD Crisis/Risk Communication Workshop: Final Report,* (Washington DC: DTRA, 2001), 10.

[32]Bill Durodie, "Terrorism and Community Resilience–A UK Perspective," *ISP/NSC Briefing Paper 05/01,* (Chatham House, July 2005): 4.

[33]Monica Scoch-Spana, "Strategies to Remedy Panic in a Pandemic: Lessons from Biodefense," *The Threat of Pandemic Influenza: Are We Ready?,* eds. Stacy L. Knobler et al., (Washington D.C: National Academy Press, 2005), 348.

[34]Durodie, "Terrorism," 5.

[35]Ibid.

[36]Erik Auf der Heide, "Disasters: Panic, the 'Disaster Syndrome,' and Looting," *The First 72 Hours: A Community Approach to Disaster Preparedness,* ed. M. O'Leary (Lincoln, Nebraska: iUniverse Publishing, 2004), 343.

[37]"President Bush: Job Ratings," PollingReport.com, January 16, 2009,

http://www.pollingreport.com/BushJob1.htm (February 12, 2009).

[38] Jessica Reaves, "Time/CNN Poll: Americans Concerned, but not Panicked," *Time*, November 9, 2001. http://www.time.com/time/nation/article/0,8599 ,183881,00.html (February 12, 2009); "USA Today/CNN/Gallop Poll Results," USA Today, November 5, 2001. http://www.usatoday.com /news/poll001.htm (February 12, 2009).

[39] Jeffrey M. Jones, "Republicans in Congress less Popular than Bush," *Gallup*, December 16, 2008, http://www.gallup.com/poll/113449/Republicans-Congress-Less-Popular-Than-Bush.aspx (March 11, 2009).

[40] Ben Sheppard G. et al., "Terrorism and the Myth of a Panic Prone Public," *Public Health Policy* 27, no. 3 (2006): 220.

[41] Janet Napolitano, "Common Threat, Collective Response: Protecting Against Terrorist Attacks in a Networked World," (New York: Council on Foreign Relations, July 29, 2009).

[42] Lawrence Freedman, "The Politics of Warning: Terrorism and Risk Communication," *Intelligence and National Security* 20, no. 3 (2005): 379.

[43] Ibid., 55-56. Note: the author also reviewed the National Strategy for Information Sharing developed by the National Security Council. One would expect some mention of RISKCOMMS; however, the document is primarily directed at improving intelligence sharing between government agencies–not sharing information with the public. National Security Council, *National Strategy for Information Sharing,* (Washington DC 2007) 1.

[44] The National Security Council, *The National Security Strategy*, (Washington DC, 2010) 18-19.

[45] This directive is still in use by the Obama administration. See the Department of Homeland Security Website: http://www.dhs.gov/xabout/laws/gc_12192 63961449.shtm.

[46] Barack Obama, *Homeland Security Presidential Directive 21,* The White House, 2007, http://www.whitehouse.gov/news/releases/2007/10 /20071018-10.html, 1.

[47] Federal Emergency Management Agency, *National Response Framework,* (Washington DC: GPO, January 2008) Pub-1, ESF-15, http://www .fema.gov/pdf /emergency/nrf/about_nrf.pdf.

[48] See Covello, et al., *Effective Risk Communication,* 161. Additionally, the author conducted informal research on the internet and was able to find additional programs sponsored by other agencies such as the Nuclear Regulatory Commission. Many other agencies, like the National Oceanic and Atmospheric Administration, have excellent Public Affairs programs that closely approximate an RC program, but are missing some key elements.

[49] Kim A. O'Connell, "Pounds of Cure," *The American City and County,* 118, no. 6 (June 2003): 8-9.

[50] Marsha L. Vanderford, "Breaking New Ground in WMD Risk Communication: The Pre-event Message Development Project," *Biosecurity and Bioterrorism: Biodefense Strategy, Practice and Science* 2, no. 3 (2004): 95.

[51] "National Consortium for the Study of Terrorism and Response to Terrorism," University of Maryland, 2010, http://www.start.umd.edu/start/.

[52]K. U. Menon, "National Resilience: From Bouncing Back to Prevention," *Ethos* (Great Britain, March 2005): 17.

[53]*Community Stress Prevention Center*, http://icspc.telhai.ac.il/main.html.

[54]Speckhard, "Prevention Strategies," 150.

[55]Peter Sandman, telephone interview with author, November, 10, 2008.

[56]Ibid.

[57]Menon, "National Resilience,"17.

[58]Sandman, interview, November, 10, 2008.

[59]Geoffrey O'Brien and Paul Read, "Future UK Emergency Management: New Wine, Old Skin?" *Disaster Prevention and Management* 14, no. 3 (2005), 354.

[60]Ragnar Lofstedt, telephone interview with author, January 8, 2009.

[61]Greater London Authority. *Report of the July 7th Review Committee,* (London, June 2006): 78.

[62]Ibid.

[63]Ibid., 81.

[64]Speckhard makes a strong case for Israel's resiliency due to excellent communications. See Speckhard, "Prevention Strategies and Promoting Psychological Resilience," 147.

[65]Health Canada, *Crisis/Emergency Communication Guidelines,* (Health Canada, Communications Marketing and Consultation Branch, September 2005) 7.

[66]Menon, "National Resilience," 17.

[67]Ibid.

[68]Ozin, "Anthrax-Euronet and Beyond," 123.

[69]Randall N. Hyer and Vincent T. Covello, *Effective Media Communication during Public Health Emergencies. A World Health Organization Handbook* (Geneva, 2005).

[70]Cleto DiGiovanni Jr. et al., "Factors Influencing Compliance with Quarantine in Toronto During the 2003 SARS Outbreak," *Biosecurity and Bioterrorism: Biodefense Strategy, Practice and Science,* 2, no. 4 (2004): 5.

[71]*Minutes of the November 8, 2005 Open Session of the Department of Homeland Security Science and Technology Advisory Committee* (November 2005), http://www.dhs.gov/xlibrary/assets/Minutes_Nov_8_05 .pdf.

[72]Michael Chertoff, "Confronting Biological Threats to the Homeland," *Joint Force Quarterly* 51, (2008): 10.

[73]Scoch-Spana, "Strategies to Remedy Panic," 332; Tierney, *Facing the Unexpected,* 259.

[74]Alan Kirschenbaum, "Does Terror Terrorize? Community Resilience in Israel," *Gazette Magazine,* 69, no. 3 (November 2007), 114-115.

[75]That said, obviously there is much to be learned for oil plans given the 2010 Gulf oil spill, but that is outside the scope of this chapter.

[76]"Appendix J: Threatcon System," *Federation of American Scientists,* November 13, 1996, http://www.fas.org/irp/doddir/dod/app-J_THREATCON.htm.

[77]"Defense Threat Reduction Agency," *Human Behavior and WMD,* 10.

[78]Sandman, interview, November 10, 2008.

[79]George Gray and David P. Ropeik, "The Role of Risk Communication," *Health Affairs,* 21, no. 6 (December 2002): 108.

[80]Michael T. Kindt, "Building Population Resilience to Terror Attacks: Unlearned

Lessons from Civilian and Military Experiences," *Counterproliferation Papers*, no. 36 (November 2006): 22.

[81]"National Response Framework," *Department of Homeland Security* (Washington DC: GPO, January 2008) http://www.fema.gov/pdf/emergency/nrf/about _nrf.pdf.

[82]Members of the Homeland Security Council include: the Secretary of the Treasury, the Secretary of Defense, the Attorney General, the Secretary of Health and Human Services, the Secretary of Transportation, the Director of the Office of Management and Budget, the Assistant to the President and Chief of Staff, the Director of Central Intelligence, the Director of the Federal Bureau of Investigation, the Director of the Federal Emergency Management Agency, and the Assistant to the President and Chief of Staff to the Vice President.

[83]Abraham Lincoln (speech, "The Gettysburg Address," Gettysburg, PA, November 19, 1863).

www.ingramcontent.com/pod-product-compliance
Lightning Source LLC
Chambersburg PA
CBHW060307290526
45789CB00001B/434